SKIING FROM THE HEAD DOWN

SKIING FROM THE HEAD DOWN

A Psychological Approach

Leonard A. Loudis, Ed.D.
and
W. Charles Lobitz, Ph.D.

J. B. LIPPINCOTT COMPANY / Philadelphia and New York

To DAD, MOM, LEE, BABS,
and especially MARCIA

L. A. L.

To FAR, MOR, JOHN, SUZY,
and especially GRETCHEN

W. C. L.

We are grateful to many people who read all or part of our manuscript and commented, cajoled, criticized, and encouraged: Gretchen Lobitz, Claude Liman, Nick Brainard, Sam Silverstein, and Joann Silverstein. Also, Herb Severson, Laura Walker, Bob Cook, Gary Gilbert, Bob Jones, Buzz Chandler, Joy Chandler, Pete Reinhart, Ken Singer, Rich Bliss, and Jim Purvis. Mike Mahoney and Kit Mahoney were particularly helpful and encouraging, making much practical advice available to us. Beatrice Rosenfeld was a fine and supportive editor and was a privilege to work with. Bertha Merriwether, typing the proverbial endless revisions, was a model of patience.

The incisive, creative reflections of Jan Helen, a superb and sensitive skier, were especially invaluable.

Finally, we want to acknowledge the contribution of our countless friends and acquaintances whose consciousness and enthusiasm for our approach, both on the slopes and off, contributed to our own consciousness and excitement.

The Authors

Denver, 1977

U.S. Library of Congress Cataloging in Publication Data

Loudis, Leonard A
  Skiing from the head down.

  Bibliography: p.
  1. Skis and skiing—Psychological aspects.
  I. Lobitz, W. Charles, joint author. II. Title.
  GV854.9.P75L68   796.9'3'01   77-12541
  ISBN-0-397-01244-6
  ISBN-0-397-01245-4 (pbk.)

Contents

Preview

Your psychology powerfully influences your skiing, your attitudes about ski conditions and terrain, and your attitudes about yourself.

Skiing is a risk sport. That is the source of your exhilaration . . . and the source of your problems. The only thing "natural" about your skiing is your innate ability to recover from loss of balance. You are neurologically wired for self-preservation; that is the only thing your body knows. Everything else—your problems, your joys, your fears, your self-criticism—is learned.

Excellent skiers do not get there by accident, and stubborn bad habits do not arise by accident. Nor does good skiing come from letting one's body teach itself to ski. Your skiing and your ski psychology are learned by way of a set of well-established psychological principles. These principles, so effective in sticking you with your problems, are equally as powerful when applied to getting rid of those problems. *Skiing from the Head Down* shows you how consciously to reapply—this time for the better—the psychological principles that led you into difficulty in the first place. This reapplication requires your active participation and involves behavioral psychology combined with aspects of Eastern philosophy: experiencing and thinking, inner and outer awareness, right-brain and left-brain activity. The approach works for beginners and experts alike and has been used successfully to enhance the performance of

17

a range of skiers, from novices to members of the U.S. Olympic Ski Team.

Recall the things you have done to learn to ski. You've probably had a series of lessons, perhaps spread over several seasons. You no doubt have gotten as many pointers as you have friends. But you may get the feeling that you have bumped headlong into the law of diminishing returns, that you are progressing at a snail's pace. In our experience, beginning now to work on your psychology of skiing—getting your head together—is like pulling the cork from a bottle of champagne. Initially this takes some effort, but then it really lets loose. In skiing, such a process dramatically opens up many new possibilities. Not only does it improve your skiing and your feelings about your skiing, but it also should clear the way for even further improvement as you learn more advanced techniques. This is what we mean by pulling the cork. And the champagne is the exhilaration. If you approach this material with the enthusiasm and seriousness with which you approach your ski lessons, we are optimistic that your effort will be amply rewarded.

Not many sports offer the incredible thrill that skiing does. As psychologists and as skiers, we will be sharing that experience with you.

CHAPTER 1

Psychology, Skiing,
Joy, and Frustration

You get up one morning and look out on a clear winter day. Ten inches of new snow! You cover the distance from bed to breakfast to mountain in three leaps and twenty minutes. The chair lift is just opening as you hit the lift line. You have to keep from diving out of the chair before you reach the top, the snow is so incredible. Blasting off down a wide-open field of untouched powder, you feel the cold, dry crystals billow around you. Each turn sends a frosty white wave over your head. You are soaring above the earth; you are diving to the bottom of the sea. Euphoria fills your lungs, rings in your ears, teases your palate, tickles your nose. Fantastic! When you get to the bottom, you turn to watch another skier dance down the field of powder, cutting tracks parallel to yours. You exchange grins of ecstasy at the end of the run, sharing your joy.

Something about skiing creates what psychologists have called "a peak experience." A good day of skiing satisfies our needs for grace, beauty, motion, mastery, danger, and acceleration. Those satisfactions keep bringing us back to the mountains day after day, season after season, and dollar after dollar.

Unfortunately, skiing is not always a peak experience. When you're having a bad day, your only peak experiences are spelled p-i-q-u-e, at best. There is no grace, beauty, or mastery when you are angry, frightened, cold, wet, or aching. Yet, that is also a part of skiing. Our experience with psychology includes both the *peak* experiences and the *pique* experiences. Most skiers that we know would like to have more of the former and less of the latter. This book is written to help you accomplish just that.

MINDFUL OR MINDLESS?

This book is also written for the skier who believes that having a brain is an asset in skiing. Unfortunately, most skiers do not know how to use their brains to help their skiing. Generally, there are two groups of such skiers, both of them frustrated: one includes the people whose heads get in the way of their skiing, and the other the people who don't use their heads at all. Both types want to improve, but they don't know how to take advantage of their brains to get the most improvement and enjoyment possible from the sport. Just as your body can learn ski technique, so your head can discover how to increase your peak experiences on skis.

What is skiing like for the people whose heads get in their way? They approach a day of skiing by *thinking* themselves into a state of near-paralysis. Before they get to the slope they worry about the weather, the conditions, and the lift lines. They contemplate taking the day off, or just buying a half-day ticket, or skiing the easier slopes. Clearly imprinted in their minds may be the falls they took on their last run yesterday, the pain of their new boots, or the size of the moguls on their favorite hills. Then, just as they are about ready to spend the day in front of the TV set, they remember all the money they've spent on new equipment, lift tickets, and lessons, and decide to swallow their fear and ski, anyway. On the way up the lift, they watch the skiers below sliding on the ice, careening off the bumps, or disappearing headfirst into the powder snow. The result is that the fear that they swallowed is now stuck in the middle of their throats. Of course, some skiers on the slope below are skiing well and enjoying themselves, but the skiers whose heads get in the way just envy them with a sigh: "If only I could ski like that." By the time they get off the lift and start their first run, they are so stiff that they are thrown by the first bump and fall in a heap of embarrassment reminiscent of their first days on skis. Then, as if their fear were not enough, they get angry at themselves for skiing like that.

What about the skiers who don't use their minds at all? Although there are generally fewer of these, some of you may be among them. They begin the day—in the words of a friend of ours—"by sending their brains out for a beer." Their brains never return. They are largely unconscious of conditions or terrain and head immediately for the expert runs. They pursue those black-diamond trail signs marked "most difficult" as though they were veins of gold ore. Without even adjusting their goggles, they blast off the first set of bumps they can find, do an involuntary half gainer in a full layout position, and, hopefully, eject from both safety bindings. They can usually be spotted after the first run: they look as though they've just emerged from a blizzard, when there hasn't been any fresh powder in a week. They are also the skiers who cannot understand why, after all the lessons they've had and all the skiing they've done (they are usually the last ones off the mountain each day), they have not improved in four years.

We realize that both these types are extremes, but we want to make an important point. There is a part of them in all of us. They represent how *not* to use our heads to get the most out of our skiing. This is not limited to beginning or intermediate skiers. Experts and competitors psych themselves out of good skiing as well.

It is hard to know how to use your head to get the most out of your skiing. You have to put a lot of time, energy, and money into your skiing. We assume that you have gotten yourself into reasonable physical shape from systematic, off-the-snow conditioning, purchased good equipment and clothing, and taken lessons from a qualified instructor. You may even have purchased some good books on ski technique. In short, you have devoted a lot of attention to how to ski with your body. Unfortunately, you have not devoted much attention to how to ski with your head. This is not at all surprising, and you are certainly not to blame. Nobody has told you that you should use your head when skiing, nor has anyone told you how to use your head. When we say "told you how," we are referring to certain specific, highly useful psychological tactics for skiing that can be taught just as you have been taught to set your edges or bend your knees. And when we say "use your head," we also mean knowing how to get it out of the way when necessary.

Until now, if you wanted to learn about skiing, you went to a ski school, and if you wanted to learn about psychology, you registered for a psychology course at a university. This means that in terms of ski instruction, a vital part of you, your head half, has been ignored. Besides, in psychology courses who ever talked seriously about skiing? This is particularly unfortunate, since there are so many recent psychological techniques that have been shown to work, often dramatically, with many kinds of people. (These include Dr. Richard Suinn's fascinating work, to which we'll refer later, with members of the U.S. Olympic Ski Team.)

This book is written for all skiers, since the techniques are useful at any level, and improvement can be dramatic at all levels. We have written it out of our experience as skiers and also as psychologists. What, you ask, do psychologists know about skiing? In general, probably no more than any other group. What we do know is something about how people learn and how they change their behavior. Since skiing is learning and changing how you behave, the principles of psychology are relevant to the sport, probably more relevant than you ever imagined. And as psychologists, we also know something about how people think. "But what does thinking have to do with skiing?" you may ask. "The last time I tried to think my way into a turn, my skis went straight into the woods." Right. You cannot intellectualize your mistakes. If all you do is think about skiing, you may as well leave your body at home in an easy chair. We are not talking about using your head as a substitute for your body. We are talking about knowing *when* and *how* to use your head to supplement your body. They work best in harmony.

SKIING IS A RISK SPORT

Psychology is important to all recreational sports, but there is one factor that, unlike golf, tennis, or archery, makes skiing more difficult to learn. *Skiing is a risk sport.* This is impressed upon you all too often when you see an unfortunate fellow-skier lashed tightly to a sled, wincing as he or she takes the bumpy ride down to the X-ray table. Can you recall what went through your head the last time you saw this happen? Do you remember how your body felt the last time you stood at the top of a steep, bumpy slope? If you wondered how you would get down, your heart raced, your breath quickened, your mouth felt dry, and your legs felt weak. Your body was experiencing all the physiological signs of fear. If you were aware of your mind, you probably noticed that it was also showing signs of fear, with thoughts like "I can't make it. Why did I take this trail? I'm not a good skier, anyway. Isn't there a cutoff around this pitch?"

There are two main difficulties with fear, even in its mild form, called anxiety. One is that it is unpleasant to experience. You know that. The other is that it interferes with learning. Psychologists know that.

Fear, Risk, Anger, Joy

Isn't risk a part of skiing? You may get a lot of kicks out of the risk in skiing. You love to go fast, to take chances. Encountering and overcoming danger is exhilarating. Skiing wouldn't be a peak experience if there weren't some risk involved. The problem for most of us is that at some point in our skiing we become *afraid.* And when we do, our skiing falls apart. There is an important difference between risk and fear. The risk is out there; the fear is inside you. The only way to avoid the risk is to stop skiing. But if you turn the fear around, you will be left with joy and exhilaration. This little equation oversimplifies, but it is worth remembering:

RISK MINUS FEAR EQUALS PEAK EXPERIENCE

We want to help you turn the fear around. The risk is up to you.

Fear isn't the only emotion that can interfere with the joy of skiing. Anger can also ruin a good day. Frustration with oneself is more characteristic of advanced skiers. Even though they have learned to love the risk in skiing, they are still susceptible to feelings of impatience and frustration when they are not skiing up to their potential.

TAKING THE MYSTERY OUT

"What a lousy day. Boots hurt. Goggles fogged up again. Gotta stop. Can't see anything, anyway. How do you ski on a day like this? Snow is terrible. Too heavy. Why am I having such a hard time on this hill? Look at that idiot. Can't believe anyone like that can ski so effortlessly. Gotta be crazy. Why can't I do that? Why am I doing what I'm doing?"

You are trying like mad to learn to ski well, but the skill is eluding you. Perhaps you yell at yourself. Perhaps you get frustrated. Maybe you're a swearer. You let loose your finest expletives, slamming your pole against a mogul that just sits there coolly. Or maybe you just cry quietly after a fall. At the same time, is your friend / husband / wife / child exhorting you to get up?

We will give it to you in one undiluted dose: from the psychological standpoint, *you have learned to ski like that.* "Wait!" you object. "I don't want to ski (or act) like that. I don't like being angry at myself. I don't like feeling frustrated. I don't like any part of it. It's not my fault. That's just the way I am!"

All you say is true, of course. You don't want to ski like that. And you certainly don't want to act like that when you ski. But you weren't born that way. Obviously, you weren't born a skier at all. Just as you've learned everything you know about good skiing, you've also learned everything you know about bad skiing—bad head habits as well as bad body habits. Knowing that you've learned it is the best realization you could have right now, because *this takes the mystery out of getting to be a good skier.* It also helps explain why, with identical technique lessons, some people progress to be good skiers, while other people don't progress at all.

As psychologists we are actually encouraged that many of your problems are head problems and can be relearned. Relearning simply uses the same principles that were involved when you developed head problems in the first place. However, the psychological process can be planned by you ahead of time and used to your advantage, quite systematically, to achieve your goals.

Relearning is a conscious process. Many people, skiers included, have trouble accepting the idea that they learned their habits, including the physical techniques for the body and the psychological habits of the mind, in the first place. "How could I have learned to do all those self-destructive things?" one of our skier friends once asked. "I didn't study bad habits, you know." That's just it. Most skiers are not actively aware of their learning, but it goes on, anyway, even without their awareness. As research in psychology has shown, we learn in ways much more subtle than we ever imagined. In our experience, many skiers do not begin to relearn until they become *aware.* That is why the relearning in this book is a conscious process. In order to ski from the head down, you first need to wake your head up.

What do we mean by relearning? We have found that skiers commonly have in mind one or more of three general goals when they say they want to learn to ski better. (This breakdown is useful even though you will notice a great deal of overlap among the goals.) (1) You may want to *increase* certain skiing skills. (2) You may want to *decrease* or eliminate some of the bad habits you have picked up. (3) You may have some strong emotional feelings or fears you would like to change.

Here are some common examples of the first goal, prefaced by "I wish . . ."

- that I could just be a little more aggressive.
- that I could ski faster.
- that I could bend my knees more.

· that I could keep my skis more together.
· that I could let my skis flow on the bumps.

Sadly, the second goal is prefaced by a futile "If only . . ."

· I could stop stiffening my downhill leg.
· I crossed my tips less often.
· I stopped yelling at myself (or my friends!).

Finally, and closely interacting with the first two goals, are those emotional changes you would like to make.

· Why am I so afraid of a slightly steeper hill?
· I don't like those sharp moguls on narrow trails.
· I wish I didn't feel so frightened of falling.
· I can't stand snowy days and flat light.

Yet, all of the "I wishes" and "if onlys" in the world are not going to help you ski better. If any of the examples hit home, you are probably aware of this truth and would rather not be reminded of it! But if you really want to improve, you will need to work with your head as well as your body, your thoughts and feelings as well as your skills.

RIGHT BRAIN, LEFT BRAIN

Thus far, we have been talking about achieving a balance between mind and body. There is another kind of equilibrium that we want to address: brain balance. You know that your brain has two structurally similar halves, the right and left brain (technically, the right and left cerebral hemispheres). In many ways, the two halves of the brain have similar functions. However, both folklore and scientific evidence suggest that each side of the brain is responsible for different functions.

Those separate functions correspond to the two sides of human consciousness, which have been a basis for the religious philosophies of many cultures. Psychologist Dr. Robert Ornstein has investigated the dual nature of human consciousness from biological, psychological, and cultural perspectives. In *The Psychology of Consciousness,* he points out that the Hopi

Indians of the Southwest draw a right-left distinction between intellectual and intuitive activity. They attribute the function of writing to one side and the function of music to the other. The Eastern religious philosophy of Vedanta distinguishes between *buddhi* (intellect) and *manas* (mind). Dr. Ornstein also points out that the Chinese yin-yang symbol expresses the bipolar and complementary aspects of human consciousness. One side represents spirit and time; the other represents nature and space.

This duality in our consciousness is also supported by medical research into the different functions of the right and left brain. The left side seems more important for intellectual, analytic work, while the right side seems more important for holistic, intuitive work. The former is associated with logic, reasoning, and linear thinking. The latter is associated with spatial relations, gestalts, and experiencing. Furthermore, research suggests that the two sides of the brain seem to complement each other in that we use one or the other mode of consciousness, but not both, at any one time (although the hemispheres do communicate with one another). This means that if you were concentrating on solving a verbal, intellectual problem, you would have more difficulty balancing on a rail fence (or skis) than if you were not. And vice versa. Dr. R. W. Sperry, in a recent scientific article, sums it up: ". . . each hemisphere seems to have its own separate and private sensations; its own perceptions; its own concepts; and its own impulses to act, with related volitional, cognitive, and learning experiences."

So what does this have to do with skiing? Recalling that the right brain is more spatial and experiential and the left brain more logical and intellectual, what happens to your skiing if you try to *think* about every motion? If you are using your left brain (linear thinking) while engaging in a physical, holistic experience like skiing, you are likely to find that you have left your coordination, and perhaps your body, at the starting gate. The effect on your skiing of *too much* thinking is characteristic of the first type of frustrated skiers we identified at the beginning of this chapter. They thought their way into a state of near-paralysis. On the other hand—or, more accurately, on the other side of the brain—a total reliance on *experiencing* without any thought at all can be equally devastating. Skiers who "send their brains out for a beer" end up cold, wet, aching, and unimproved. However, a combination of left- and right-brain activity can lead to some pretty gratifying experiences on skis. As one of the authors relates:

One of my amateur races in the East was an opportunity to compete in the North American Alpine Championships. On the day of the slalom, I was excited but a little intimidated since many of the other racers had more natural ability and more experience than I. When I saw the course, I wondered if I wouldn't be a lot happier sitting in the lodge, sipping a hot buttered rum. The hill was extremely steep and the turns so tight that the course seemed designed for midgets. I felt myself start to get tense. "This is ridiculous," I thought to myself. "I'm doing this because I enjoy it, so what's to get so uptight about? If I didn't belong in this race, I wouldn't have been invited." (Without realizing it, I was using positive self-talk to control my anticipatory anxiety.)

I turned my attention to learning the course. Every section demanded concentration, rhythm, and caution. "Don't go for broke on this one. The whole course is a killer. Smoothness is the key. The speed will take care of itself. Especially on the bottom part. There are too many times when you've blown a good run by losing concentration and crashing near the bottom," I told myself. I was really *thinking* about this one, planning my attack against a course that could trip me up at every turn.

I loosened up by making tight, smooth turns above the start. I felt good. I had planned my strategy in my head. Now it was time to start experiencing the rhythm I wanted. I didn't know it at the time, but I was now shifting my activity from my left to my right brain. When I got in the starting gate, I wasn't thinking at all. My concentration was on a rhythmical experience. When I pushed out of the gate, it was smoothness all the way to the finish. I felt great.

The other racers didn't fare so well. Skier after skier blasted off the course or tangled himself in a forest of poles. No strategy, no rhythm. After the first run, I was in sixth place, one and a half seconds out of first.

I studied the second course. It was like the first—steep, tight, treacherous. "Same story, same strategy. Go for rhythm, not for speed," I thought. I crossed the finish line feeling like a ballet dancer. It was fantastic. When the race finished, I was a total of eight-tenths of a second behind the winner. Fourth place. No medals, but a lot of satisfaction. I had beaten a lot of better skiers. And I had beaten the course.

There is a time and a place for left-brain activity in skiing. There is also a time and a place for right-brain activity. We *think* both are necessary for skiing from the head down. We've also *experienced* the necessity of both. Our intent is not to emphasize one side of the brain over the other. We don't intend to perform psychosurgery on one half of your mind by suggesting that you "tune out" your thoughts or disconnect your experiences. Your brain works best if it is left intact. Our purpose is not only to help you integrate your thoughts, feelings, and experiences so you can use your mind to help your body, but also to help you utilize the unique contribution of each half of your brain.

COMING ATTRACTIONS

The next two chapters define and illustrate the common head problems that skiers, including ourselves, are prone to. We discuss the psychological basis for these problems, with an emphasis on taking the mystery out of how you learn both good and bad habits. We separate the relearning process into its elements. This breakdown is artificial. We make it because it is necessary to enable you to specify your own problem areas, understand why they are maintained, and design an efficient way to change them. Your clear understanding of your problems *and how you got there* is powerful information to have when you choose to begin the change process. You will recognize yourself (perhaps painfully!) in parts of these chapters. On the other hand, all of our individual psychologies are different, so some examples may not apply to you.

Chapter 4 initiates you into the formal effort to work with your skiing psychology. It describes the change process. In Chapter 5, the action begins, starting the process of waking your head up to your skiing. The remaining chapters deal with the psychological techniques involved in skiing from the head down. They are not just a collection of ideas or hunches. Some of them have evolved from laboratory and clinical work by a great many psychologists. Other tactics come from our work on the ski slopes. They represent the merging of our experience as skiers and our knowledge as psychologists.

In the end, we take your skiing as a total experience, without obsessing or overanalyzing, and especially without intellectualizing. We want you to let go, to feel, to be aware of your relationship with the mountain in space and time. We view skiing as a flowing process. This is right-brain stuff. It all fits together as an entire experience, a gestalt, an integration of your body and mind that, when working right, seems almost spiritual in its beauty and grace. We feel it is an intense individual challenge, a communication between a lone skier and a mountain that is itself as complex in variety as you are in your feelings and thoughts and ways of skiing.

CHAPTER 2

It's Frightening What Fear Does to Your Skiing

Watch young children rocketing joyfully through the bumps. They are as close to being "natural" skiers as anybody can come. Even when falling down, they display little of the awkwardness and hesitancy that are characteristic of adult skiing. Why are children so much looser than adults? First, as we grow, our bodies become less resilient, making it more unpleasant for us to fall. When children do a half gainer into a snowbank at ten thirty in the morning, they do not feel crippled for the next couple of runs. Nor do they immediately think they ought to go in for lunch or retire to the whirlpool bath. They do get discouraged, but their discouragement usually comes as a result of being cold, bored, or lonely. They are not discouraged about their skiing.

Second, we develop what is euphemistically termed "discretion," but more accurately called "fear." When you "risk" yourself, when you put yourself into the position of losing your balance and potentially falling, many involuntary systems within your body take over. This isn't an idea or an opinion, it is a neurological fact. Your nervous system is wired up that way. What it boils down to, of course, is that humans are "wired" for self-preservation. Many of the ski positions in which you find yourself are unstable, especially if you are a beginner. It's as true when you're learning to do your first parallel turn as it is when you're skiing your first deep powder.

When you are unstable, the vestibular system in your inner ear detects that you're losing your balance. You respond involuntarily. You reflexively experience a stiffening of your muscles. At the same time, you most likely get a "rush": among other things, your heart will speed up, you will breathe faster, adrenalin will be released into your bloodstream, and blood will be shifted to your major muscle systems. In other words, you experience an emergency reaction.

ENTER PSYCHOLOGY

Humans don't just absorb sensory stimuli; we actively process our experiences, responding to the world and our bodies as we perceive them to be. Each of us, of course, sees the world differently. One skier may perceive the "rush" experienced when almost falling as just that and no more. This person says to him- or herself, "Wow! I almost fell; I could feel my body beginning to stiffen. . . . Just relax. Get under control again." If you can do this, you are the exception. Most skiers don't react with this kind of equanimity despite the fact that this interpretation is the accurate one. You did almost fall. What you experienced was the rush that normally accompanies loss of balance, and it can be perceived as such without imagining potential catastrophes. As you'll see shortly, those few skiers who interpret experiences this way are ahead of the game.

The more typical response is something like "Whew, that was close. Could have been a bad fall. Might have broken my neck or something. Got to be more careful." This second reaction is the one that gets in the way. You have rehearsed in your mind how dangerously close you came to falling, how bad the fall could have been (or how bad the fall actually was). You have, in fact, increased the fear and the apprehension. You've increased the probability of being tense. And you have certainly increased the likelihood that the feeling will occur again, often with increased intensity, the next time you're in a similar situation, which may be only thirty more feet down the mountain! We will go even further than saying that this second reaction is the more common one; based upon the way people have learned to respond to threatening situations since childhood, it may well be the normal one. *That is why it is so inefficient for your body to "teach itself" to ski. As far as your body knows, tensing up is the normal neurological response to being unstable.*

As happens with all of us, your body and your mind get all mixed together. Your body may do the same thing on or off skis that the next person's does. But your mind is different. In this example, your body has reacted naturally and reflexively to a loss of equilibrium. Your mind said, "Close call! I've got to be careful." Result: your head has plugged in a memory that losing your equilibrium equals being afraid. The next time you almost fall, you reexperience the "fearful" thought, and you become more tense and more cautious. In a short time, you become a skier of the utmost "discretion."

There are two crucial points about skiing psychology that we want to make here:

1. You can learn a great deal from technique lessons. You can also learn a great deal by observing other skiers. (Learning by observation—what psychologists call modeling or vicarious learning—has a powerful influence on our behavior. We'll return to this in Chapter 9. The point to be made here is that even modeling probably won't work efficiently to improve your skiing if you don't first work on your head.) If your head says that the reflexive stiffening of your muscles (the normal response, remember) signaled a close call (danger), then your mind has gotten in the way of doing what you wanted it to do. That is why you so frequently say to yourself, "Now why can't I do that? I know what I'm doing wrong. I just need to bend my knees more!"
2. You have now set yourself up for a terribly self-defeating conclusion: "If I know what I'm doing wrong and still can't do it right, I'm never going

to learn how. I'm just *no good.* I have awful balance." This is what we call the Self-defeating Syndrome.

These two points are a prime cause for slow improvement
in your skiing. Look for a moment at how you got there. Based
upon your "evidence," you've made the logical conclusion.
But based upon the real facts, you have not reached the correct
conclusion. Your evidence was that you could see what others
were doing that you were not. Since you found you couldn't
just let your body do what it should, you concluded that something must be wrong—namely, you. Then you blamed yourself
and called yourself "hopeless."

The real facts are, however, that you have ignored what
fear has done to your skiing. Review the critical points. The
only natural thing about learning to ski is the reflexive (automatic) response humans have to a loss of balance. The response
is an emergency tensing of the muscles—for example, stiffening of the downhill leg, leaning into the hill, tautness of the
musculature of your torso. Along with that, you have responded with the predictable psychological fear reaction, and
the response was a *natural* one. Finally, you have taken a solid
step toward psyching yourself out.

EMOTIONAL LEARNING

Thus far, we've been discussing what is called "emotional
learning." Your reflexive responses and most of your skiing
feelings, like fear, are the result of this type of learning. Here
is how it works. You experience the tensing that occurs when
you have the emergency reaction. The reflexive reaction has
occurred under a certain ski condition. It may be a sharp
mogul for some of you, heavy snow for others, gaining too
much speed for others. The point is that it has occurred in
conjunction with a certain stimulus, that is, a certain ski condition.

Let's say the stimulus is a short series of sharp moguls. In
psychological terms, the emergency reaction has been paired

with that ski condition since they occurred at the same time. You reflexively tensed up those muscles on the moguls. After several pairings of your reflexive emergency reaction with that stimulus, the sharp moguls will come to cause the tenseness *even without your losing your balance.* Thus, when you have had frightening experiences with certain snow conditions or types of runs, those conditions or runs will cause you to feel tense even before you get to them. All you have to do is *see* the moguls. Where it was a normal emergency reaction before, through emotional learning it has now become a learned psychological response. Furthermore, conditions only moderately similar can also produce feelings of apprehension. And, as if that were not enough, simply imagining the situations can cause apprehension.

Consider for a moment the implications of this kind of emotional learning. Here you are, about to take a run. You make your first turns. Just ahead is one of those stimuli that have become capable of causing you apprehension—for example, that series of moguls. You see them coming. You tense up and hit the first mogul stiffly instead of flexibly absorbing it. Whether you realize it or not, you have *learned* to do the exact opposite of what good mogul technique requires.

Thus, the fear cues you have learned (which are different for all of us) have become a real problem: (1) they involuntarily caused a tensing of your muscles, and (2) they caused a tensing of your mind. When your mind is tense, you fail to think realistically. You tend to think about potential catastrophes and ignore your body, your skis, and the terrain. And all of it was *learned* in a most normal and predictable way.

OPERANT LEARNING

Where emotional learning has to do with reflexive responses and feelings about skiing, operant learning has to do with skiing behaviors. Skiing obviously involves a series of voluntary physical behaviors. Setting your edges, bending your knees, and unweighting are all examples. You do them intentionally. You think about them until they have become almost reflexive.

Operant learning, the learning of these voluntary behaviors, is largely dependent upon what kind of payoff you get for skiing the way you do. Does skiing that way look better? Does it give you a feeling of balance and grace? Such payoffs can be positive benefits. The thrill of a good powder run, a compliment from your friends, the sensation of setting your edges and beautifully carving a turn—all of these are positive. It makes sense that you will probably try to repeat these skiing behaviors on the next run. They have worked for you. You felt good.

Of more concern here, though, is the subtle way that fear influences your ski habits—in other words, how fear influences operant learning. Along with many other skiers, you have probably never taken the time before to analyze how you acquired your good habits. It should now be easy to see how the positive result of a particular skiing behavior would tend to keep you skiing that way. You have received a genuine payoff for doing it—for example, that compliment or good feeling.

But what about your bad habits? Why do you keep avoiding that steeper slope or that field of moguls? Why do you persist in leaning too far into the hill? What possible payoff can there be for persisting with the stiff downhill leg when you know it is not right? The answer is a major part of ski psychology, and it has to do with the unfortunate but persistent effects of fear. It is based upon the same principles as those applied to good skiing habits and again has to do with payoffs: *the effects of fear creep in whenever your payoff is that your behaviors help you avoid or escape some part of skiing that is unpleasant.* Anxiety and fear, even embarrassment and humiliation, are like that. If there is something you can voluntarily do to decrease your discomfort, doesn't it make sense that you will probably go ahead and voluntarily do it? After all, who likes to be uncomfortable?

It may make excellent sense, but it certainly does not make excellent skiing! Some examples of voluntarily avoiding discomfort would be the following:

- Staying on the easier hills most of the day. Thus you avoid the apprehension that accompanies the moguls, steep slopes, or whatever situation makes you tense up.
- Always stopping to your right (or left), thus avoiding uncomfortable feelings of instability when stopping the other way.
- Not doing a kick turn on steep terrain. Instead, you probably plant your poles way below you and awkwardly step around. By doing this, you avoid the fall you anticipated if you had kick-turned.
- Never skiing under the lift, even though it may have the best snow. This way, you avoid the imagined humiliation you'd suffer if you should fall.
- Traversing across that heavily moguled hill, arms flailing, each bump throwing you further off balance. Because you successfully avoid falling every so often, you tend to be stuck with the problem.
- Rotating your shoulders back into the hill in response to your feelings of instability.

We've come to another critical point on how your psychology influences your skiing. Notice that in each example the fear, uneasiness, and embarrassment you are avoiding are your own feelings. You carry the payoffs around in your head every time you ski! Their influence on your skiing habits cannot be overestimated. In each case, the actions you have taught yourself are exactly opposite to what you should have done. Notice, too, that you are avoiding something that has been the result of earlier emotional learning. *The major reason that bad habits are so agonizingly persistent is that you are carrying around in your head the payoffs that maintain the bad habits!*

Stop for a moment before moving on to some of the points that follow. If it is not clear how emotional learning (your feelings) influences your operant learning (your voluntary behaviors), go back and reread the examples. Then make up some of your own. What is the first bad habit that comes to mind? Define it. What do you see as the payoff for doing it? Does it decrease or avoid apprehension, or feelings of loss of balance? To work on your skiing psychology, you need to understand how your psychology works on your skiing. Thinking up your own examples is one of the best ways to do that.

BAD HABITS SEEM FOREVER

It may seem to you that the bad habits should just go away. In fact, they are terribly frustrating, make you angry with yourself, and lead you unfailingly back to the old Self-defeating Syndrome.

From a psychological standpoint, there are three interrelated reasons for this resistance:

1. The payoffs that maintain the bad habits are in your head.
2. Because you are getting a payoff for what you are presently doing, it is not likely that you are going to work on new tactics.
3. Your present bad habits work only every so often to "save" you, despite your hopes that they will work every time.

Let's look at these three points more closely. The first one should be clear, but we'll give you a different example just to be sure.

Herb and Bonnie were enjoying a fine advanced hill. Dropping over a crest onto a steep pitch, Bonnie skied beautifully through some deep snow between the trees. Herb literally stopped in his tracks, looking for a way around. Not finding one, he slowly skied the rest of the pitch. His body was stiff, and he fought to keep his balance.

The payoff in Herb's head was his avoidance of falling and the lessening of his feelings of apprehension. By skiing slowly, stiffly, and miserably, he succeeded this time. In contrast, it never entered Bonnie's head to slow down, because her earlier emotional learning was somewhat different—there were no payoffs for slowing down.

The second point is also illustrated in the above example.

Herb didn't try anything new! Bonnie was yelling at him to face more downhill, but he was still twisted back into the hill, feeling safer that way. He was angry at himself, but at least he wasn't falling and he was feeling safer. Had he relaxed his muscles and looked ahead, he would have done better. When you try new things for the first time, they will always feel a little odd and you will be unstable. That is even more reason to revert to the bad habit. Essentially, you have been punished for trying something new! It is hard to convince your mind that "Nothing ventured, nothing gained." And that is particularly true in skiing.

To illustrate the third point, suppose that skiing tensely through the trees, shoulders uphill, legs stiff, saved you *all* of the time. You wouldn't be "hoping" it would save you. You would know it did—and every time, at that. Then, after this device worked every time to keep you from falling, suppose it suddenly began to fail. It would take very few failures before you changed your style. But, in fact, your bad habits do not work all of the time. You get used to their failing some of the time. They persist because they work just often enough that you hope, as soon as your feelings of apprehension start, that this time they will work again. And perhaps, unfortunately, they do.

If you doubt our analysis thus far, ask yourself why there are so many bad habits that seem almost universal. Emotional and operant learning are taking place and interacting. We will say it again: skiing isn't natural. Your responses to loss of equilibrium, and the resultant learning of the bad habits we all seem to share at one time or another, are what is natural. This is part of the psychology in skiing that skiing from the head down is designed to change.

VICARIOUS LEARNING: LEARNING BY LOOKING

Almost everything you learn by direct personal experience can also be learned by watching other people. There is an abundance of solid evidence in the scientific literature that we can and do learn both operantly and emotionally by observing others.

> Susan had just skied an intermediate run in and out of some chopped-up powder. She was feeling great, practically alone on that part of the mountain. Stopping at the intersection of two intermediate hills, she watched three reasonably good skiers take falls on a pitch just ahead. They were visibly shaken by the experience. Susan skied cautiously and tensely down that pitch, looking for all the world like a beginner not enjoying herself. Yet the pitch was no steeper, no bumpier, no choppier than the stretch she had just finished.

What happened here was that Susan learned vicariously by watching several people model fear on that pitch. It got her emotional self going, which, in turn, made her physical self tense to avoid falling. This is a fine example of the subtle ways in which we learn. Susan couldn't figure out why she couldn't relax on the second pitch. She was unaware of the vicarious learning that had just taken place.

Learning by observation is powerful indeed. Clearly, this can be both good and bad. For years, instructors have recognized the good with their comment, "Watch me." But it can also be bad. Recall that it is an essential part of the Self-defeating Syndrome. In that situation, an instructor or friend saying "Watch me" could conceivably do more harm than good if the suggestion triggered such thoughts as "I can never do that" or "I'm awful." Also, many skiers model fear. Others model some pretty terrible habits. All of these spell exactly as much trouble as the direct learning of bad habits, and they work in basically the same way.

How about the good side? Can learning by observation really be of help? Absolutely and emphatically yes. There are techniques designed to help you maximize the good and minimize the bad. (We'll review these in Chapter 9, "Vicarious Learning: Extra Instruction at No Extra Cost.")

GETTING COLD FEET

There is one additional negative side effect of feeling apprehensive when you ski. It is an aspect of the fear response that invariably goes unrecognized by skiers: being scared or nervous when you ski tends to make your extremities more susceptible to cold. There is an interesting physiological basis for this phenomenon.

The part of your nervous system that is involved with feeling emotions, with involuntary bodily responses like digestion and heart rate, and with preparing the body for action or relaxation is called the autonomic nervous system. It is divided into two physiologically distinguishable parts, the sympathetic and the parasympathetic. In general, these two parts act in opposition to each other. The sympathetic usually sends out the impulses for your anxiety or emergency reactions, and the parasympathetic sends out impulses associated with relaxation.

The sympathetic gets your body ready for something. Your heart rate speeds up, your breathing changes, your mouth gets dry, and a lot of blood is sent to your major muscle systems. When that blood gets shifted to your major muscles, there is vasoconstriction in your extremities, and the blood supply to your hands and feet is lowered. Now you're in a bind, literally as well as figuratively. When you experience anxiety and your peripheral blood vessels constrict, it is obviously going to be more difficult to keep your extremities warm. The expression "getting cold feet" didn't just pop up from nowhere: because you're afraid, your sympathetic nervous system has "sent orders" to reduce the blood flow to your feet while increasing that flow to your major muscles. Keeping your hands and feet moving helps, of course, but you are fighting your nervous system if you're anxious and trying to keep warm at the same time.

In contrast to the action of the sympathetic aspect of your autonomic nervous system, the parasympathetic is associated with relaxation. Among other things, there is an increase in blood flow to the extremities when you are relaxed. In fact, accurate measurement of skin temperature at the fingertips is used in some types of psychotherapy both to assess the presence of anxiety and to help teach people relaxation skills. If you ski psychologically relaxed, your hands and feet will probably stay warmer.

Notice that we are not claiming that because you get cold hands or feet you must be fearful. (When you get really seriously chilled, there is an involuntary shift of blood to reduce heat loss and to try to keep body-core temperature at acceptable levels. This also involves a dramatic shifting of blood from the extremities but is not the same thing we have been discussing regarding anxiety.) We are saying, however, that if you don't ski relaxed, not only will it be more difficult to ski well, but you will be a lot colder while you are standing there frustrated!

CONVERSATIONS THAT HURT YOUR SKIING

Let's turn to how talking to yourself has such a powerful effect on your skiing. There are portions of your brain that developed early in human evolution that are most important in the physiological response to emotional experience. As strange as it may seem, it is quite literally difficult for those portions of your brain to distinguish between self-generated emotional input (like simply *talking* to yourself about fear) and input from your *external* environment. You can and do respond to your internal "fear-talk" about those sharp moguls in a manner very similar to external "fear-stimuli" (the actual moguls)! You can and do respond to anger with yourself and to self-punishment in a manner similar to punishment directed toward you by another person. That is why it is both physiologically and psychologically possible for your skiing to seriously suffer when you are your own worst enemy.

CHAPTER 3

On Being Your Own Worst Enemy

One of the authors recalls an experience two years ago. It started as a two-day stop at Steamboat. The first day was spectacular. The second should have been even better.

Ten inches of light powder had fallen beginning late the preceding afternoon, and ended with a brilliant sunrise.

The second day began with a ten-minute wait for a breakfast table and a thirty-minute wait for food. I started muttering to myself: "Powder's going to be tracked up. I should have gotten up sooner. . . . Dammit, where is our food? There's no excuse for this kind of thing. Can't stand waiting for other people to do their job. . . ."

My friends stayed relaxed.

We proceeded to the lift, finding a fifteen-minute line. "I can't stand waiting in line. The snow is too incredible. I've got to have some space," I thought.

My friends stayed relaxed.

We got to the top of the mountain. With my finely tuned hypersensitivity that day (wrong side of the bed and all of that), I kept muttering to myself: "Snow's tracked. . . . Like an anthill up here. . . . I'm a fool for not getting up earlier. . . . My boots don't feel so hot, either." All of that in spite of the fact that only a dozen or so people were ahead of us on this particular run.

My friends stayed relaxed.

We started down the mountain. I fell in the first hundred yards. I was enraged: "Damn bindings. Too many people, too."

43

My friends had their rhythm. They were flowing beautifully over and around the bumps. The powder was spectacular. They reluctantly stopped and waited a few hundred yards down the mountain. Picking myself up, I skied fitfully down to them and started complaining. I was really into it. I couldn't stand myself or my skiing.

To make a painful story short, I continued with the same attitude for the rest of the morning. By early afternoon, my friends were telling me to get lost—I could yell at myself and wallow in my own misery if I wished, but I was ruining their skiing. I felt miserable, getting worse with every run, and totally insensitive to my body and the terrain.

You have heard the expression "to be your own best friend." It usually means to be good to yourself, both physically and mentally. It means having reasonable expectations, complimenting yourself, and talking to yourself in a positive way. Each of these things improves the quality of your life. Each also improves the quality of your skiing a great deal more than you are probably aware.

With distressing regularity, we neglect to be our own best friend. Instead, we become our own worst enemy—and not just in skiing, either. Even day to day, this is often one of the biggest problems we create for ourselves. (There is an increasing body of research and clinical literature in psychology concerned with modifying "worst-enemy" habits.) Skiing is one of those areas where being our own worst enemy stands out in bold relief. We get angry with ourselves. We talk nonsense to ourselves. We frighten and punish ourselves.

To understand the unusual power of what you imagine and say to yourself, you need to appreciate the fact that it is difficult for your autonomic nervous system to distinguish between the world "out there" and the world you create "in your head." Recall that your autonomic nervous system is associated with your emotions and tends to respond to your "experiences" automatically. It matters little to your autonomic nervous system whether these experiences originate in your external environment or your internal environment. (Technically, they don't become "experiences" until you have received and processed—talked to yourself—about your sensory input.) You can (and frequently do) talk yourself into feeling "emotional." You have demonstrated that principle to yourself many times. Recall the last time that you felt jealous by simply "thinking" that someone special to you was with another person. Other examples abound: puckering up when thinking about a lemon, feeling turned on by sexual thoughts and images, and so forth. All the "feelings" you had at those times are the responses of your autonomic nervous system to your self-talk and your images.

CONVERSATIONS AND IMAGES

Actually, there are at least two internal "channels" to which your autonomic nervous system will readily respond. Since they significantly influence your emotional responses while skiing, it is well worth defining them. They are the two channels of "imagining" that many people use (some people report they favor one channel, some the other). In skiing, the same two channels operate both to psych yourself out *and* to psych yourself up:

Channel 1: *Conversations* you have with yourself "in your head." These are usually called "self-statements," "self-talk," "private monologues," or "covert verbalizations."

Channel 2: *Images* of events, mostly visual, but including the other senses in varying degrees. In skiing, for example, common problem images involve "seeing" or "feeling" yourself crossing your tips and crashing.

It doesn't matter which channel you typically use. The important point is that your self-talk and images have an amazing influence on your feelings and behavior. *You* begin and continue the monologues and images *on your own*. In fact, in skiing (and living), we often set ourselves up for failure. The ideas of "it's in your imagination," "it's all in your head," or "you're imagining things" are crucially important in looking at human behavior. Recall the last time you were told, "Don't worry. It's all in your head!" If you are like most people, that did not help your feelings in the least; you still worried, even though it may have been only in your head.

There are two kinds of destructive self-talk in which you may engage (remember that we will be using the term "self-talk" to include visual images as well as statements you make to yourself): (1) anger-talk and associated self-punishment, and (2) fear-talk and associated catastrophizing.

> Marti felt self-conscious about her ski outfit. Gary felt the same way about his five-year-old skis and boots. Both were standing around having conversations with themselves that included these types of comments: "I wish. . . . Oh, I dunno, but this stuff seems out of it. What's that guy there skiing on? . . . Wish I had those, he must really be good!"

> Debbie was a classic when it came to throwing internal temper tantrums. A talented skier, she'd lose it occasionally in deep powder, slam her pole down (sometimes losing it), and get so angry with herself that the lightest powder would seem like cement: "What a fool I am! I just can't get this. What's wrong with me? I ought to be able to do it. I really should be able to relax more."

Does this sound familiar? When skiers talk about "psyching themselves out" or their "heads getting in the way," they are talking about being their own worst enemy. *You are your own worst enemy* when your self-talk is angry, self-punishing, self-critical, or fearful. On the positive side, you are *psyching yourself up* when your self-talk is positive, rewarding, euphoric, or complimentary.

ANGER AND SELF-CRITICISM

Let's look first at the effect that anger and harsh self-criticism have on your skiing. To put it in perspective, a brief exercise is helpful:

> Recall an instance when you were angry with yourself. Precisely why were you so upset? If on skis, was it because of falling or "chickening out"? Take a few minutes to sit back and recapture that anger.

Reconstruct as accurately as possible your comments to yourself. What were you saying? How did you feel while you were blasting away at yourself? Were you swearing a lot, perhaps?

Now, *repeat* it all to yourself. *Do it.* Get into and recapture that self-talk. Create a wave of anger. Feel it. Hear yourself talking. Hear yourself swearing. You're angry at yourself. Stop reading for a moment and let it pour over you.

Now, for the final step, turn the tables. Recreating the feelings you have just had, ask yourself quite seriously *how you would have reacted had someone else said the same thing to you in the same tone of voice, for the same reasons.* Sit back and imagine it for a moment. How are you reacting? Feel like telling them to go to hell?

To understand the effect this type of imagining can have on your skiing, consider this carefully. How long do you think you could or would remain friends with someone who criticized you as much as you do yourself? Not long at all, we would wager, especially on skis. *To punish yourself and to expect to like yourself or your skiing just isn't possible!* It is a ridiculous assumption. Yet it is clear that you set yourself up, catching yourself between the proverbial fire hydrant and the dog, with an apparent single-mindedness that would do credit to a true masochist. At that point, *you have psyched yourself out.*

The Effects of Self-punishment

Exactly what specific effects, you may ask, does self-punishment have on your skiing? It has some of the same effects that punishment does in general. It makes you feel terrible, both about yourself and about your skiing, and it gives little information about what is the appropriate skiing strategy, which leaves you helpless to do anything different.

Bad feelings toward yourself create immediate problems. Most obviously, you may decide skiing is no fun. We wonder how many people are on the verge of giving up skiing, not because they get particularly cold, or even because they fall a lot, but because they have made skiing so unpleasant by self-punishment that it has ceased to be fun.

Obviously you have not given up skiing or you wouldn't be reading our book. More likely, only certain conditions or runs have come to be no fun. In any case, you are psyching yourself out. You are reacting to your internal private conversations with yourself and *not* to what is really happening "out there." For example, no one is *really* yelling at you, and yet your autonomic nervous system does not "know" the difference. *Therefore, your feelings don't, either!* To the degree that you are responding to your skiing with anger and self-punishment, skiing is controlling you. You are the effect of your skiing. That is obviously the reverse of the way it should be. Filling your head with severe, unfocused self-criticism leads directly to decreasing sensitivity to your body, your skis, and the terrain.

In addition, self-punishment teaches you *nothing new* in terms of technique. When you get angry at yourself, just as when someone in your external environment punishes you strongly and consistently, you tend either to become paralyzed or to flail about, trying anything that holds even a remote prayer of working.

The same thing applies when you punish yourself for your skiing: you learn what will *not* work for you, but the punishment alone tells you exactly nothing about what *will* work for you. So in addition to making yourself unhappy, you have learned nothing new! As if feeling bad were not enough, you are into a cycle where you give yourself increasing reason to feel bad and to swear at yourself. This, in turn, maintains your pathos. "I can't ski this. What's the matter with me, anyway?" leads to more bad feelings and more tension. These lead to worse skiing, and even further justify (in your mind) more self-punishment.

Finally, you have not built in any payoffs for the continuation of good skiing tactics. You know well by now that with no payoffs, even parts of your skiing that *are* good will not be likely to continue. In fact, if you have a couple of excellent ski behaviors tucked in among a few bad habits, and you tend to be a self-punishing person, the chances are increased that even the good habits will stagnate.

SELF-CRITICISM AND STANDARD-SETTING

In skiing, particularly, your *expectations* or *standards* create a severe problem. More accurately, failure to meet your expectations gives you a real cause for self-punishment.

Pete always started off a day of skiing absolutely high on the weather (no matter what it was), his skiing companions (they could practically have been chosen by chance), and the area he found himself skiing for the day (often determined only by a flip of a coin). He personified the enthusiastic, optimistic recreational skier. He did, however, have a problem: by early afternoon his optimism and enthusiasm were severely strained, and by the last run he was crabby as hell. What's worse, he couldn't figure out how he lost his enthusiasm every day.

He would discuss the problem over some wine and cheese in the bar at the end of the day (some wine and cheese in *any* bar would invariably revitalize him). He had a common problem. Pete, it seemed, would start off the day saying he was going to ski every run with what he liked to call "flowing aggression": "I will not get tense. I will flow over every bump, setting edges, carving turns, rarely falling. My legs will be like shock absorbers."

But he never achieved "flowing aggression." How could he expect to? He had started skiing only late the previous season! As a result of repeated failures to meet his expectations, he began to get angry, then depressed, and finally felt like giving up altogether. He would do that day after day!

Standards. The word sounds innocuous enough. In fact, however, it is inextricably tied in with the entire self-criticism issue. Some of us "fail" to meet our standards a small percentage of the time. Others "fail" a large percentage of the time. The difference in "failure" rates lies not so much in skill levels as in the goal-setting process. It is the standards you set for yourself that to a great degree determine how successful you are. If your expectations are unrealistic, you will fail often. You become a self-punisher *and then turn right around and set the standards equally high the next time.* You predictably "fail," go through your now-familiar self-criticism routine, and let your skiing *control you* in the next fifty feet as well.

The price you pay for your expectations is high. It does not matter whether you are a novice or an advanced skier, your standards can still cause problems. As you respond to your repeated "failures," you effectively block any reasonable chance for efficient learning. You give yourself no new information about skiing. Furthermore, *you are not having any fun.*

FEAR AND CATASTROPHIZING

"The only thing we have to fear is fear itself." President Franklin D. Roosevelt's famous comment is as applicable to skiing as it was to the economic crisis of the Depression. Fear is an autonomic nervous system response to external or internal (self-generated) stimuli. The effects of fear on your skiing are now familiar:

- Fear is an integral part of the Self-defeating Syndrome.
- Fear often gets "attached" to certain skiing conditions (emotional learning) and makes you insensitive to your body, your skis, and the terrain.
- The reduction of your fear is the payoff for avoiding new tactics.
- Fear feels terrible!

However, we have yet to discuss some problems with the self-generation of fear. The self-generation of fear is, of course, a large part of psyching yourself out.

We have said that the autonomic nervous system does not distinguish between internal and external fear situations. You can scare the hell out of yourself, or something can scare the hell out of you. There is another critical question, however:

Why do the *same* external situations, certain ski conditions, for example, affect one person and not another? Why should some skiers love fresh powder on steep hills, and others quake in their boots when faced with the identical situation?

Much of the answer to that question lies in the *self-generating* process: the Stoic philosophers of ancient Greece did not have to be skiers to observe that *we respond to the world as we perceive it to be, not as it objectively exists.*

Look at a field of big, steep moguls. Scared? Or are you challenged? It is clearly the same mogul field, either way. The moguls are not entirely responsible for making you feel scared or challenged. In large part, *you* are. Thus, we had better look to our self-generation of fear if we are to understand it.

Just as in the self-punishment process, internal fear-talk will be provoked by certain conditions in your environment. The self-punishment cycle may be started by setting a goal and "failing"; the fear-talk may be started by just momentarily losing your balance, actually falling, observing another skier falling, or simply by just imagining that you're falling. At that point, you will begin to catastrophize. The process of catastrophizing involves thoughts and images about what *might* happen or *could have* happened. (Broken legs? Broken skis?)

Catastrophizing is self-defeating in that you are again attaching labels and emotions to ski conditions and terrain *before you even get there.* As you are lying after a fall on the lee side of a mogul, you are not fearful because you just fell. You have already fallen, so there is nothing to be afraid of. Rather, your fear is that you *may* again fall in the next hundred feet. Alternatively, you may be rehearsing in your mind what *could* have happened (the "Whew-that-could-have-been-an-absolute-disaster" routine) and be responding to that.

IT'S NOT ALL BAD

Lest you have the impression that all internal talk is bad, we want to make it clear that it is equally powerful when you use it to your advantage. Skiing from the head down, after all, does not mean that you are under the control of your skis; it means your skis, *and your head,* are under *your* control. Self-talk can help your skiing with the same power that it harms your skiing.

Gymnasts, ski racers, and many other professional athletes actively modify both their conversations with themselves and their images during practice and competition. Downhillers ski and "memorize" a course, running it many times in their head. The U.S. Olympic Ski Team currently is coached in these techniques. In his book *Ski in Six Days,* former Olympic silver medalist Billy Kidd tells us that he used the techniques to particular advantage in the 1970 World Championships. Due to an earlier back strain, he had actually limited himself to skiing the downhill only three times prior to the race, about one-fifth of his usual practice runs. But he had *observed* other racers practicing and had *mentally* rehearsed the course many, many times. It worked well. He placed fifth in the downhill in that race.

The influence of your self-statements, images, and perceptions is powerful; some of the techniques covered in the forthcoming chapters will teach you to use that influence to dramatic advantage.

CHAPTER 4

S.K.I.: The Process of Active Awareness

Many years ago, when travel in northern New England was accomplished by narrow two-lane roads, a New York ski enthusiast was motoring to Stowe, Vermont, for a weekend of spring skiing. Never having traveled these roads before, he was worried about losing his way. His anxieties were realized when he came to an unmarked fork in the road next to an old general store. Fortunately, a weathered Vermonter, his corncob pipe smoldering in his mouth, was sitting on the porch of the store. "Old man!" hailed the New Yorker. "Which way to Stowe?" "Well, sir," the Vermonter replied in his best Yankee accent, "you best take the right fork here and go up to the four corners. Head north and uh. . . . Nope, on second thought, better take the left fork and go up to the next village. . . . Whoa, that ain't it, either. You better take this road on back to the covered bridge and head east till you. . . . Nope, come to think of it, mister, *you can't get there from here!*"

Skiing without awareness is like putting yourself in the hands of the old Vermonter. You may know where you want to go, but you don't know where you are, and you aren't likely to find a way of getting there. Active awareness is what differentiates the conscious skier from the mindless one. It is what allows you to take charge of your skiing, to look at it, see it, change it, and make it yours. In short, it is what allows you to become the *cause* of your skiing rather than the *effect* of it.

53

To be the cause of your skiing, you need to *know* how you are skiing. Knowing is being conscious. (Even the word *conscious* derives from the Latin word meaning "to know.") Knowing involves experiencing and thinking about what you've experienced. That means using both halves of your brain, the right/experiencing half and the left/thinking half. To get where you want to go, you first need to know where you are. In skiing, knowing where you are means sensing and *feeling* your skiing. This is the work of your right brain. You need to feel the snow, the terrain, the movement of your body, and the edges of your skis.

"Knowing where you are" is necessary *but not sufficient* for "getting somewhere." You still need to know where to go. That requires *thinking* about your skiing. This is the work of your left brain. You need to think about what is presently influencing your skiing, what you want to accomplish, and then decide the best way to get there. This means being conscious of what works and what doesn't. The process of *active awareness* involves knowing with both sides of your brain. It involves *experiencing* and *thinking* about what you have experienced.

S.K.I.

Active awareness is the central theme of skiing from the head down. It is a short sequence of steps. The process of moving through these steps, and the result of doing so, enables you to get in touch with your skiing and with your ski psychology. It enables you to set your goals, to establish your personal challenges. Finally, it is the basis for deciding which tactics presented in the remainder of this book are to be the most helpful in meeting your challenges.

Here are the three steps:

S = Sensing. Be aware of and let yourself experience what you are doing and feeling when you ski. We view this sensing as primarily a right-brain function. You may be bashing down a hill, or you may be lying there after a fall. You may be making a tensely determined effort to ski slowly, carving each turn, or you may be worrying about crossing your tips. *Sense,* without comment, your skiing. *Sense,* without comment, the psychological space you are in. You are noticing what is going on in your body and in your mind.

K = Knowing. This is the thinking part, the left-brain activity. What are your problems, your personal challenges? *Knowing,* in active awareness, means thinking systematically about where you are with your skiing so that you know clearly, not vaguely, where you wish to go.

I = Inquiring. What triggers your skiing? What triggers your head? What are the cues and the payoffs in your skiing that produce your fear, anger, or euphoria, and that maintain your skiing habits? This inquiry will form your basis for designing change.

Awareness means S.K.I.-ing; active awareness means being involved in your skiing. As we go along, we will suggest ways for you to use both halves of your brain *actively.* Skiing from the head down is a participation sport. We are inviting you to participate in the process of developing awareness. From here on, you have a chance to do that actively with us. We will be suggesting ways for you to know your skiing and ways for you to change what you don't like—from the head down. We call these suggestions "exercises" and "processes." The exercises are things for you to practice. They are ways for you to get your mind in shape for skiing. The processes don't require any practice. They are ways for you to increase your awareness of different aspects of your skiing. Some of the exercises and processes can be done while you are reading this book; others require you to be on your skis.

SENSING

Consider your skiing. What are you aware of? If you're like most people, you would respond with something like "I'm good," "O.K.," "Lousy," "Expert," "Advanced beginner." Those are classifications of your skiing. We're not interested in how you "class" yourself.

We would like to suggest a process designed to move you toward discovering the senses in your skiing. All that this process requires of you physically is that you sit comfortably in your chair, or wherever you are right now. The process works best if you have your arms and legs uncrossed and your eyes closed. We will instruct you when you need to close your eyes. During these processes, and the others that follow in the book, you will be relying on your ability to reexperience events from your past. This requires you to imagine that you are doing certain things. You may already be good at imagining, or you may not be. If you have ever daydreamed, you already know something about imagining. The only difference is that imagining is *focused* daydreaming.

Sensing Your Senses

To warm up your senses, you first need to warm up your ability to *perceive*. This means using your *different* senses. Start with your sight. Look around the room and notice all the different shapes and colors. Look at a piece of furniture. Try to see its shapes, colors, and textures as though you were noticing it for the first time. Don't classify what you see. For example, don't say to yourself, "That's a blue chair" or "That's a brass lamp with a brown cord." Just look at what's there without pigeonholing it.

Now use your ability to feel. Sit down, close your eyes, and run your fingers over a texture near you: the arm of your chair, a tabletop. Notice the feel of it, notice its temperature. . . . Be aware of how your clothing feels against your body and your feet in your shoes, the tightness of a belt or underwear, the material of a shirt or blouse against your back, arms, and shoulders. Notice the position of your body. Don't look at it, *feel* it. . . . Notice how you are supporting yourself. Be aware of which muscles are tense and which are relaxed. Move your body with your eyes closed and notice the changes in your muscles and the feel of your body against your clothes and chair.

Turn your attention to your hearing. With your eyes closed, listen to the sounds in the room. Change your body position and notice the sounds of your movement.

Now focus on your sense of taste and sense of smell. Be aware of the tastes inside your mouth. Notice the smells in the room. Don't try to figure out *what* you taste or smell. Just notice it. Take time to experience all your perceptions and sensations. If you found yourself rushing through your senses, go back and play with them. Enjoy them.

Sensing Your Body

Once you have thoroughly experienced your senses, you are ready for a little practice at sensing your body. We have found many skiers who *think* they have good body-sense, but by trying this exercise find it could use some fine tuning. You probably know someone, perhaps yourself, who makes a few turns and then asks a fellow-skier, "Hey, how'd I look?" That question comes because your perceptions are out of touch with your body. When you're conscious about your skiing, you can feel how you look. In fact, you can feel without looking at all. Do you recall the last time you skied in really flat light or, even worse, in a "white-out"? Remember how awkward you felt? Nobody can ski well in flat light, but some people do better at it than others. This is a vivid example of the importance of a finely tuned body-sense. It is necessary in all of your skiing.

Go ahead and try this:

Close your eyes and stand up. Without reaching back, sit down and try to feel your body moving to meet the chair. Keeping your eyes closed, stand and sit several more times. With your eyes still closed, stand up and jump from side to side with your feet together. Roll your knees to the inside of each jump. Keep trying to sense where your body is moving. Be aware of whether you're landing in the same place on your jumps to either side.

Stand in front of a stairway. With your eyes open but without looking at your feet, jump up to the first step with your feet together. Jump back down. Repeat this several times until you have a feel for the way your feet are moving up to meet the step and back down to meet the floor. Then try it with your eyes closed. You should be able to feel if your feet are going to meet or miss the step. As a second exercise, stand at the bottom of the stairs with your eyes open and jump up each step with your feet together. Don't look down at your feet. The faster you are able to do this without looking down, the more awareness you have developed for the movement of your body. (This exercise is also a good muscle conditioner.)

Here is a third exercise. Start on the sidewalk at one end of a block, perhaps with a friend. Close your eyes and walk briskly ahead. How far do you get before you step onto the grass or (if your friend has a grudge) into a tree? With practice, you will be able to lengthen that distance. In fact, the more you practice these exercises (and others you can make up that are similar), the more awareness you will develop.

The next time you're on skis, stand on the flat and jump from side to side with your feet together, rolling your knees to the inside. Then do it with your eyes closed. It will feel more awkward because you are not used to feeling your skis and body move together, but this is also excellent practice.

KNOWING: PINPOINTING YOUR OBJECTIVES

Describe two or three problems with your skiing that you would like to overcome. These goals should be realistic. They should also be specific enough to be manageable. There are two reasons why your goals should be specific. First, if you can't accurately specify the improvements you would like to make, you will only be able to guess which tactics to use for change. And if your attempts at improvement are just guesswork, you will still be a victim of the unfocused and unconscious learning that taught you your bad habits in the first place. Second, if you can't specify your goals enough to keep track of them, you won't be able to tell if you're improving. And if you don't know whether or not you're improving, it will be easy for you to get discouraged, feel like giving up, and go back to being your own worst enemy.

If your goals are "To be a racer" or "Ski bumps better," you have plenty of company, but these answers are too vague. What aspects of being a racer? Better than what? Almost all of us have a habit of making our standards too vague and setting them too high. We defeat ourselves before we begin. This is how we set ourselves up to be our own worst enemies.

> Carol was not satisfied with her skiing. She had broken her leg early in her first season. Her second and third seasons were totally fear dominated. Her goal was not to be afraid.

There is no doubt that Carol had a problem with fear. But her definition of the problem wasn't adequate. Fear of what? Speed? Bumps? Ice? Should she have included internal fear-talk? How about her predisposition to sit down and cry when things went bad? When you pinpoint a problem area, you need to be specific.

> Since she had broken her leg shortly after losing control one day, she could vividly imagine it happening again. In fact, she began thinking about it a couple of days before planned ski weekends, occasionally imagined it while riding the lift, and consistently reminded herself how long it had taken to recover from the first break. While on the hill, she fought every small

gain in speed by long traverses. Her goals were to ski more aggressively while on easy hills and stop the rehearsal of potential catastrophes that served only to scare her.

That is much clearer. When asked what she meant by "more aggressively," she defined it even further as "skiing a little faster and more down the fall line." What she meant by "scaring herself" were her internal statements about loss of control and broken legs. This was something she could monitor easily by paying attention to her self-talk.

Another example:

> Jim was a good, aggressive skier. His technique was sound, and in general he was happy with his skiing. Most of his friends looked to him as an excellent skier, except that he fell a lot. His goal was to ski from the top to the bottom of any typical advanced run under conditions of chopped-up snow without falling.

This was not a very workable goal to start with. Jim could certainly monitor whether or not he fell, but what would he learn about *how* he did it? What *specific* problem prevented him from skiing top to bottom without falling? By not properly defining and working with those specific problems—a common error skiers make when wanting to "improve"—Jim did two things. First, he learned little about what his problems really were and what strategies to use to attack them. Second, perhaps worse, he set standards that were too high for his initial efforts. As he failed to meet those standards (because they were unrealistic in the first place), he increasingly became his own worst enemy and critic. In those snow conditions, he began to psych himself out in the truest sense of the words. He needed to develop more awareness of his falling.

> Jim observed that he was crossing his tips and falling forward most of the time. He found he was not particularly fearful, but quite embarrassed to ski like that in front of his friends. He was also extremely—in fact, unreasonably—angry at himself. He would have internal temper tantrums at the same time he was trying to ski those conditions. He was stiffening up and losing track of his weight distribution. So he modified his goal

to: first, work on his self-statements of embarrassment and anger; and second, begin with a few relaxed turns and move up from there.

Jim's goals, though still not the best if we are going to be supercritical, were definitely more realistic and workable than skiing top to bottom without a fall. He could have been more clear about "relaxed turns," but he felt he knew what he meant. He could have gone on to define "relaxed turns" as paced breathing, smoothly absorbing the bumps, or even humming to himself. In any case, his new pinpoint and definition were workable.

Take a moment now to review the necessity of clearly KNOWING. It is probably apparent that if you are not conscientious at this point, the rest of your effort will be jeopardized. That is the least of the hazards that result from carelessness in this step. At worst, you will try a couple of times, fail to change at all, throw this book in the trash basket, and give up. You will, of course, have acted predictably. Why continue when there is no payoff?

We are exquisitely aware of this potential problem; that is why we put so much emphasis on being conscientious. At this stage, the only argument we can give you about the naturalness and power of this approach is to remind you of how powerful the identical learning principles were in originally sticking you with your bad habits. Later, as you *conscientiously* reapply these principles, your payoff should be obvious. Just as positive payoffs maintain your good skiing habits, so will they encourage you to maintain your development of skiing from the head down.

To KNOW is to define and pinpoint your problem(s), remembering that your definition should be realistic, and should involve specific skiing actions and feelings that you can continue to be aware of. Included would be things like

- almost always avoiding steeper hills
- sitting too far back on your skis
- not bending your knees
- telling yourself how stupid you are

· burying your tips in powder
· traversing too much

but not so nonspecific as

· losing it in the bumps
· being afraid of skiing
· wanting to ski better
· wanting to look good

Sometimes you may feel you need to start with a fairly general definition, perhaps even some of the nonspecifics above. That is O.K., providing you realize that as you examine the problem you will have to specify it before you can do anything about it. In order to develop active awareness, you start with general impressions from your experience and refine them down to specific, manageable problems. That is part of being your own "personal scientist" (see Chapter 5). You will be amazed at how many of your problems can be distilled into something workable. And you will be delighted to find how much easier it is to improve when you have some specifics on which to focus. It is like the difference between going to the doctor, saying, "I don't feel well," and telling him or her, "I have a pain in the lower right part of my abdomen that gets worse when I move." The doctor's task is much easier in the latter case.

INQUIRING: THE CONTEXT OF YOUR SKIING

Once you have identified an aspect of your skiing that you want to improve, *you must expand your awareness of the problem by inquiring about the context in which it occurs.* Your skiing has two contexts, outer and inner. The *outer* context includes all those aspects of your external environment that influence the way you ski—the snow, weather, terrain, people, your clothes, even your skis. The *inner* context includes everything you carry around with you—your thoughts, sensations, feelings, memories of past experiences, and your self-talk. You need to inquire about the contexts in order to change your skiing. *Different contexts produce different problems in your skiing and require different solutions.* Recall that Jim (in the previous section) was falling a lot. He focused on the outer context to discover what precipitated his falls.

> For Jim, chopped-up fresh snow resulted in multiple falls. It also evoked feelings of embarrassment. By paying attention to his skiing *and* his falling, he made an interesting discovery: he fell a lot more when he was skiing with other good skiers. (As you might expect, his feelings of embarrassment were also greater when his friends were present.)
>
> When Jim turned his attention to the inner context of his falling, he became aware of a pressure to show off for others. While his body was contending with the terrain, his mind was focused on who was watching him. Out of the corners of his eyes, he would check to see if people were looking at him. Jim realized that he was not skiing the mountain, he was trying to ski the crowd.

Once the context of a problem becomes clear, a variety of solutions, based upon the tactics covered in the forthcoming chapters, begins to unfold.

Inner and outer contexts exert a powerful influence on your skiing. It is easy to let yourself become the victim of your skiing. If you are in that psychological place, you have surrendered all of your control to outer contexts such as gravity, weather, and terrain, and to the vagaries of your inner context (an unfocused mind or a mind focused on self-defeating thoughts and images). The way to reassert control is to develop awareness about how you function in response to your contexts. Then you are in a place of awareness and knowledge and moving to a place of coping and control.

PUTTING S.K.I. TOGETHER

Here is a final example of a problem that is well described by a skier who had developed a high level of active awareness.

> Don is a college racer who had always skied well in slalom and giant slalom but had trouble maintaining his speed in the

downhill. Although he was in superb physical condition, he always felt weak and exhausted at the end of every downhill race. He had had such poor times in the last few downhill races that he was in danger of being dropped from the ski team.

By reviewing his last few races in his mind, he discovered that he had no trouble with high-speed turns; as long as the course was smooth, he stayed relaxed and maintained his momentum. On the other hand, he realized he was physically tense on straight, fast, bumpy sections of the course. Even *imagining* himself on a bumpy race course resulted in his becoming tense and gripping the arms of his chair. The next time he practiced a downhill run, he noticed that he actually held his breath and clenched his teeth as he entered a bumpy section. The result was that instead of flowing over the bumps, his skis banged into every undulation in the snow, costing him precious time. By paying attention to his skiing, he realized that holding his breath and tensing his muscles occurred every time he skied bumps at high speed. No wonder he was so exhausted at the end of every downhill course!

Don was able to pinpoint his problems by using S.K.I. as his route to active awareness. First, he *sensed and experienced* (right brain) what was happening inside his body (tight muscles, clenched grip on his poles, locking his knees in one bent position, not breathing). He did this by focusing all his attention, *without comment,* on what his body felt like during his downhill practice runs. He did not focus on "going fast" or "holding a perfect line" through the turns. His *only* objective during these runs was to SENSE his body. We want to stress the importance of this single focus. Don would not have been able to pinpoint his tension and breath holding if he had been concentrating on his "line," his "speed," or any other focus except his senses and his body.

The second step in Don's process of discovery was to KNOW where he wanted to go. In his case, it was reasonably straightforward: less exhaustion, and increased relaxation, including regular breathing. Notice he did not say, "Decrease my time." That would not have given specific information.

Don then INQUIRED about his contexts. In analyzing the tension, he noticed that it occurred in some contexts and not in others. Specifically, it occurred immediately preceding and during bumpy sections but not on smooth sections. Finally, Don adopted the tactics in the remainder of this book which are designed to meet his goals.

A COUPLE OF AIDS

The more you *experience* your body's sensations, the more you will know and notice ("know-tice") about them. For example, you may not be aware of whether or not you ski with a stiff downhill leg or with your shoulders rotated into the hill until you sense those parts of your body when you ski. Similarly, the more you listen to your head, the more aware you will become of your statements to yourself. For example, you may not be aware that you cause your inability to ski on ice until you listen to yourself mutter, "Dammit! Why can't you edge on this stuff? These skis are lousy, anyway."

Realistically, we know that you will not become instantly aware of what your body and head are doing and feeling. As we have emphasized, the more you pay attention, the more active awareness you will develop. Fortunately, you do not have to do this alone. There are several ways of getting external feedback on your skiing. One of the best aids is to ask a friend to notice some things about your skiing. Usually, when people ask their friends, they say something like "How'd I look?" That produces a response of "Great," "Not bad," "Funny," or "I don't know." In other words, it produces an evaluation. Let us reemphasize that feedback of this type is not helpful. A better way to get useful feedback is to ask your friend a specific question—for example: "Am I sitting back on my skis?" Even better, ask for a comparison between how you feel and someone you see: "I feel like I'm sitting way back on my skis. Do I look like that skier over there?"

Ski instructors can be particularly helpful in giving you feedback. They can *show* you what you should look like. This not only helps you pinpoint your bad habits, it can also give you a model for good habits (see Chapter 9).

Another source of external feedback is photography, either still or motion pictures, or even videotapes. Photography can serve as a cue for your active awareness of your body posture. That may make it easier to identify a particular problem impeding your improvement. Take a look at some old pictures or films of your skiing if you have them. Notice whether you look tense or relaxed, balanced or awkward. Compare them with ski-technique pictures from a skiing magazine. Then, the next time you go skiing, notice whether you *feel* the way the picture *looked.*

If you don't have any pictures or films of your skiing, take a camera along the next time you go. Or have your picture taken by one of the ski photographers on the slopes in many areas. They can have your pictures ready the next day. Some areas are experimenting with videotape recording. For a modest fee, you can ski a section of the slope, stop at a replay monitor, and get instant feedback on what your skiing looks like. Also, more and more areas are utilizing videotape feedback as part of their ski instruction. As psychologists, we are familiar with the power of immediate feedback to facilitate learning. Having a certified ski instructor with you to direct your attention is ideal.

A word of warning about self-observation, whether through videotape or photography: most of us are so goal-oriented rather than process-oriented that we immediately categorize everything into "good" or "bad." Our tendency in viewing a picture is to give ourselves a grade, as though that were the end of it. Yet, the purpose of self-observation is to identify your strengths and weaknesses so you can build on the former to improve the latter. It is not to grade yourself "A" through "F," or "good" through "bad." So when you observe yourself, save the final grade until you have hung up your skis for good. In the meantime, SENSE, KNOW, and INQUIRE with openness.

Contrary to the words of the old Vermonter, you *can* get there from here!

EXERCISES

The processes included in this chapter dealt with knowing your senses and feeling your body. You will now find it useful to go through the active-awareness process, using S.K.I. for an entire skiing sequence. Read through the paragraphs that follow. Then uncross your legs, close your eyes, and relive the experience we describe.

> As you sit comfortably, you are going to recreate an experience of *graceful, exhilarating, joyful skiing*. You will be combining elements from your own experience. They may all be from the best day of skiing you ever had, or they may be from different runs, different mountains, or different seasons. Don't try to force the elements together. Just focus your awareness on the skiing experiences you have had. Let them come together in any combinations that occur. Imagine that you are dressed for skiing. Be aware of the feeling of your gloves, the poles in your hands, your feet in your boots, the feel of the snow under your skis as they slide along. Feel the cold air in your lungs and the breeze in your face. Notice the scenery, the color of the sky. This is a fantastic day for skiing.
>
> You are starting on the best run you have ever had. Feel yourself turning gracefully, your skis carving, your edges holding. Let the rush of joy build inside you. You feel challenged by the conditions and the terrain, and you are skiing it magnificently.
>
> Now close your eyes and continue to reexperience the run or runs. Keep experiencing all the good skiing that you have had until you reach the bottom. Then open your eyes. . . .

Take a few minutes to think about the elements in your positive skiing experience. What kind of terrain? Steep or flat? Bumps or smooth hard-pack? What kind of turns were you making? Long, smooth traverses off the fall line, or quick, short turns? How was the visibility? Were you with others or alone? How were you dressed? How was your body feeling? Tight and quick? Relaxed and smooth? What thoughts or ideas were going through your mind? Sense. Inquire about contexts. Keep reviewing all the elements of your good skiing until you have a clear idea of how, what, where, and with whom you ski when you're skiing well.

Now tune up your senses and go through the S.K.I. sequence with an unpleasant skiing experience.

> Turn your awareness back to your past experiences. You are going to recreate an impression of *awkward, frustrating skiing.* As with the positive experience, you will be combining elements from your own skiing history. Don't try to force any elements together. Merely recall, without comment, the negative skiing experiences that you have had. Let them come together in any combinations that occur.

> Imagine again that you are dressed for skiing. Be aware of the feeling of your gloves and the poles in your hands and your feet in your boots. (They may even feel too tight or too loose.) You're not enjoying yourself. You may be too hot or too cold. You're wet from having fallen too many times. This is a lousy day for skiing.

> You are starting on the worst run you have ever had. Feel yourself turning awkwardly. It is as if your skis had a mind of their own. Every turn is a struggle. Let the rush of anger and frustration build up inside you. You feel overwhelmed by the conditions and the terrain, and you are skiing it miserably.

> Now shut your eyes and continue to experience the run or runs. Keep experiencing all the miserable skiing you've had until you either reach the bottom or give up in a heap of frustration.

Now take a few minutes to KNOW the elements in your negative skiing experience. Review all the conditions, terrain, types of runs, body sensations, and thoughts until you have a clear idea of how, what, where, when, and with whom you ski when you're not skiing well. These may include bad physical habits, self-blaming thoughts, or emotional reactions like fear or anger. These are the weaknesses in your skiing, maybe in your life as well. Some of them are things you want to change. In this "bad" experience, be in touch with KNOWing. Where are you, and where do you wish to go?

You may have had some difficulty recreating these scenes. The difficulty is related to the novelty of applying an active-awareness process to skiing. It would be useful to go through these exercises several more times, at least until you can come closer to S.K.I.-ing in your imagination.

CHAPTER 5

Prologue to Change

A great deal of psychological research has shown that the tactics involved in making your desired changes are based on relearning—by using exactly the same psychological principles as were involved in acquiring the problem in the first place. It doesn't matter that many of your problems originally evolved from emotional learning related to your "natural" responses; it doesn't matter that many of your problems progressed "naturally" from your physical and emotional learning into self-defeating syndromes and "worst-enemy" habits. The fact that the psychological principles were so remarkably effective in saddling you with your bad habits originally shows that the principles work. The essential and most encouraging point is that the same principles can be reapplied, systematically and consciously this time, to meet your skiing goals. *Skiing from the head down is the systematic and conscious reapplication of the psychological principles that were involved in acquiring your problems in the first place.*

The key here is "systematic and conscious reapplication." We want to be clear about this: the reapplication of those psychological principles is an active affair. You do not simply "blank your mind" or "let your body take over." Your bad habits amply demonstrate that in a risk sport your body does not naturally teach itself. Too much previous learning has taken place. (It may have begun with your mother's admonitions to "be careful, you might hurt yourself.") To change your habits, a conscious relearning process is necessary. This means active mental involvement: participation in discovering what is maintaining your bad habits, learning to relax so you can develop good habits, not being your own worst enemy, and not catastrophizing. Consider professional athletes—gymnasts or skiers, for example. Most will tell you that they *actively* work on their heads, psyching themselves up by having thoughts incompatible with potential catastrophes, by "actively relaxing," by mentally rehearsing their moves to learn new skills. With few exceptions, they can ill afford to let their body teach itself. Nor can you.

MORE THAN ONLY "GOING FOR IT"

We would like to caution against a couple of things most of us seem to share when we undertake to apply these principles.

First, once you have identified two or three weaknesses in your skiing and have described them clearly, choose the one that is the *easiest* to work on. If you are like most of us, you will probably want to tackle the hardest one first. That would be setting yourself up for failure again. There is no need to create frustration for yourself. Yet, some people insist on doing just that by attempting to ski *over* their heads instead of *with* their heads. For example, we have a friend with that attitude who is determined to master skiing big moguls. Every chance he has, he takes off for the biggest field of moguls he can find and literally beats his brains out against them. So far, the score is Bumps—50, Brains—0.

There is a second common mistake that you may make when you want to improve your skiing: you may try to change everything at once. Think back to the last time you took a lesson or read a book about skiing. The next time you went skiing you probably told yourself a half-dozen things to remember on your first run: "Keep your knees flexed. Don't stiffen your downhill leg. Hands forward. Weight on your downhill ski. Hips and shoulders square. Don't lean into the hill. Angulate. Get forward on the steep. Use your edges." And so on. There was so much chatter going on in your head that you had one of your worst days.

In order for your body to respond, your mind needs to be focused, but not obsessive. You cannot be trying to accomplish six things at once. This principle is so simple and so obvious that we often forget it. The easiest way to maintain a single focus is to *take one step at a time.* Choose *one* problem to work on first. Once you are satisfied with your improvement, start on another problem. As you build on your improvements, the overall structure of your skiing will emerge. It is like building a house. Imagine what the structure of your house would be if you tried to lay the foundation, put in the windows, paint the walls, and wire the electricity—all at the same time.

BE YOUR OWN "PERSONAL SCIENTIST"

Skiing from the head down, as you now know, requires careful sensing, careful thought, and a reasoned exploration of your problems. You are developing awareness about the way you are currently skiing, both with your body and with your head, so you can identify what works and what doesn't work for you. You are to be systematically applying physical, emotional, and cognitive relearning procedures to change what doesn't work into what does. This process will let you be your own "personal scientist." (This is the term used by Dr. Michael Mahoney in teaching people the skills to work on the problem areas they feel need change.)

We don't mean that you will become a white-coated scientist sitting in a laboratory with test tubes and a blackboard covered with intricate equations. As your own personal scientist, you will be exploring the mind-body relationships in your own experience. You will also be changing your head and body habits to bring your skiing more under your own control. The remainder of this book focuses on that process.

One last word about being your own personal scientist.

Science, whether personal or universal, can become boring if it is approached mechanically and without curiosity. On the other hand, it can be exciting and stimulating if it is approached with an enthusiasm for discovery. As you take off on your exploration of your mind and your skiing, adopt an attitude of curiosity. If you find yourself losing interest, it is probably because you have lost that curiosity about your skiing. We have discovered that whenever we become bored with our skiing, it is because we have already become bored with our psychology. We are either trying to force our bodies to do something our minds aren't ready for or we have stopped being active with our minds. There is a lot for you to discover about how your head affects your skiing and what *you* can do to affect your head. Don't push it. That leads to anxiety. Don't become unconscious about it. That leads to passivity. Especially, don't "work" at it. Take an interest in it. Let your curiosity make a "sport" out of psychology. You are on the verge of making significant progress in your skiing.

CHAPTER 6

Handling Problems by Operant Techniques

Meet Dexter M., IV:

Dexter, being a fourth-generation M., was a rather proud soul. He was a fine tennis player, exceedingly competitive business person, and a hard-driving, beautiful skier. At least, under certain conditions he was a beautiful skier. (He was always, however, proud and hard-driving.) His nemesis, his most acute personal embarrassment, his most dependable producer of self-punishment, was the supersteep. He freaked. And the more he freaked, the more he pushed. The more he pushed and failed, the more he harassed himself. His private monologues centered on his incapability of making long series of smoothly linked turns on those supersteep bump runs. He made, instead, a long series of roughly linked recoveries. Each bump would throw him farther back; he would stiffen, swear, stiffen some more, recover, swear—and continue driving from top to bottom (it worked well in business; why shouldn't it in skiing?).

"O.K.," he finally said to himself, "I'll take it one step at a time, probe with some active awareness, and change this idiocy." He did exactly that. He focused on the problem, felt his body stiffen while his head was spinning with self-punishment, and was able to clearly pinpoint his difficulty. Specifically, he always began his series of recoveries after the first two or three bumps and just kept on pushing.

At that point, he began to inquire about his contexts. What preceded the problem? Only sharp, steep bumps. He would stop at the top of the pitch, contemplate the bumps, grit his teeth with determination, and go. The first few would cause automatic efforts to regain his balance. That hint of stiffening, in turn, brought on the punishment and self-statement to keep pushing: "I can, I will, I am going to do this if it kills me, keep going, keep going. . . ." This was followed by increased determination to push harder on the next run. And the cycle would begin again.

There are several tactics in skiing from the head down that zero in on problems similar to Dexter's, or like the fear problems Carol had. They are based on the principles of operant learning that point out that your skiing, both the good and the horrible, is not an accident. You learned it; it is being cued by certain conditions; it is being maintained by certain payoffs; and the psychology *can* be changed.

Since the operant learning of skiing is considered voluntary, you can bring it under control by doing one or both of two things: (1) Change antecedents—that is, those contexts that *cue* you to ski and think in a certain way. This can be accomplished by changing your exposure to those cues or by changing the "value" of the cue. (2) Change consequences—that is, change the payoffs you get for skiing as you do. This can be approached by eliminating the payoffs entirely, or by increasing the payoffs for better skiing habits in conjunction with decreasing the payoffs that maintain your own personal embarrassments.

It would be so gratifying if skiing were a straightforward matter of learning the physical skills required. Then you could just take lessons and "go for it." Your head would never get in the way. Your payoffs would be that those physical skills always worked to let you turn with grace, float exquisitely through the powder, and flow like mercury through the bumps. Each of us would ski our fantasies. Instead, we see errors that are universal. We see stiff legs, a death grip on poles, and awkward falls. We see skiers out of control coming to a stop with relief, skiers standing on top of steep pitches contemplating disaster. These are the obvious errors. We also see the finest skiers, the true experts, getting angry with themselves, seemingly unable to master "that problem," a problem often so subtle and so far beyond the skills of the average skier that it usually goes unobserved.

So the world is not all that easy. But psychological strategies to modify some of our antecedents and consequences, the subject of this chapter, do go a long way in our efforts to meet our personal challenges. The strategies are straightforward and, we have found, immensely helpful—*if* they are used systematically and with consistency. If they are not used consistently, the price you pay is frustration and an *increase* in the power and persistence of your nonconstructive bad habits. On the other hand, if you are consistent and systematic, the changes that you will experience in your skiing as a result of changing some of these skiing behaviors are going to surprise even the most optimistic among you. We could say that the cost-benefit ratio is very much in your favor. (It is interesting to note that psychologists have shown that when your *behavior* changes, your feelings and emotions often follow. That appears to be working backward—don't we do things because we "feel like it"?—but in fact it is the case. It is partly for this reason that operant-learning tactics have a great influence on the emotional parts of your skiing.)

CONTROLLING YOUR ANTECEDENTS

Let us turn first to control of antecedents. You can consistently change your exposure to the personal contexts that control your head and your skiing. Here is an example of an almost universal tendency of skiers to let the mountain ski them:

The "Lookers"

Imagine yourself skiing along a trail, perhaps one that is familiar to you. You know that there is a steep pitch, a rather sudden change in terrain ahead. You arrive at that spot. Recreate that scene right now. What do you do next? What is going on around you? If you are like most skiers, you stop! You join several people contemplating the pitch ahead, perhaps overhearing a comment or two about the bumps or the skiers halfway down. You have let the mountain ski you, and in doing so, you have made a cardinal, easily changed error: *you stopped at precisely the wrong time.*

Like other errors in skiing, the stopping was "natural." It was a predictable occurrence, especially among beginning and intermediate skiers. You have probably been opening up on the easier stuff that preceded it, and it is natural to slow down with a change in your environment. You are contemplating an event that is somewhat anxiety-arousing before you tackle it. (This latter point is reflected in folk expressions such as "gritting your teeth" or "grin and bear it.")

There are problems with this seemingly innocuous habit. First, you have lost whatever rhythm and forward motion you had. Second, as you are standing there, mulling over the pitch ahead, you have plenty of peace and quiet to be your own worst enemy. Listen to yourself. What are you saying? Is it self-generated fear-talk? Whatever it is, you are likely to be cognitively rehearsing (thinking about and imagining) the *worst.* Third, you may be observing some skiers on the way down ahead of you. Let's suppose they are struggling. What are you saying to yourself? What are you rehearsing about how *they* must feel? Or suppose the skier is good, executing her turns beautifully, pointing her skis down the fall line and really flowing. What are you saying then? Most likely: "I wish I could do that!" or "Damn, she's good!" Perhaps you even make some such remark to another skier standing a few feet away.

You must stop psyching yourself out. How does physical learning relate to that? Simple. *Control your antecedents. Don't stop at the crest of a steep section.* Slow down, perhaps, if it is a blind pitch, but retain your movement and rhythm. The antecedent that you discover during your active-awareness analysis is the terrain change. You were under what is called *stimulus control* when you stopped. The pitch, the moguls, and the people all "conspired" to trigger your "worst-enemy" dialogues, your involuntary emotional arousal, and your observational learning.

So, one thing Dexter did whenever possible was not to stop at the top of the steep. His wasn't a problem of fear, but rather that the pitch cued a determination, a gritting of his teeth, a tension throughout his body that set him up for being thrown back in the bumps. This, of course, would trigger even more tension. He began to make a dent in that cycle by giving himself less opportunity to grit his teeth with that tense determination.

Let's take a moment to dismiss a couple of replies skiers have made to these suggestions. First: "I stop because I'm tired when I get there." If you know that the pitch is coming, and you feel you will be too tired to continue when you get there, stop significantly above it and rest. Then reestablish your rhythm, relax, and ski over the crest. Second: "I have to stop on steep hills." If you feel you must stop when skiing the steep, do it after you have some rhythm, a hundred yards or so over the pitch. You can certainly psych yourself out there, too, but it is somewhat less likely—particularly if your first several turns were good. Besides, it quickly becomes rewarding to ski right past all the Lookers at the top of the pitch.

How much more straightforward could a skiing-from-the-head-down tactic be? It requires only the systematic alteration of a voluntary "natural habit." Now you are beginning to ski the mountain.

The "Stoppers": From Weakness to Rhythm

Here is another "natural" error that skiers make, one that is also found among very fine skiers and can be tackled by a simple operant-learning strategy. Imagine for a moment that you are skiing one of your favorite hills. You have nice rhythm, are executing some delicious turns. All of a sudden you catch an edge, get thrown back on your skis, get a real "almost-falling" kind of rush with the reflexive tensing of your muscles. Now, recreate that incident. What do you do next? Imagine that sequence, and imagine what happens then.

If you are like most skiers, you *stop!* You think back on the close call: "Damn, that was close, must have caught an edge." Or you slam your pole against the snow in frustration: "I'm awful." And so forth. Though your script may be slightly different, you are making the behavioral error of stopping at precisely the time you should be regaining your balance and rhythm. Just as stopping at the top of a hill puts you under stimulus control, so does this error (a "natural" response) set you up for inappropriate cognitive rehearsal. It is an antecedent inviting catastrophizing, and it teaches you nothing. Even the best skiers sometimes lose control, of course, but it is the intermediate and beginning skiers who are most likely to come to a full stop. It is an error inviting the self-generation of fear (and anger, too, if you are feeling frustrated), an error that you can least afford to commit at that point. (Chapter 12 offers important pointers about what *is* appropriate cognitive rehearsal under these circumstances.)

But there is another, equally damaging result: learning to regain control is just not possible when you habitually stop from a position of weakness. One of our cynical nonskiing friends describes learning to ski solely as the process of gaining finesse in your recoveries. When you have so much finesse that the world cannot detect your recoveries, you are a good skier. We wouldn't go that far, but learning recoveries is clearly part of skiing. Coming to a full stop, instead of learning recoveries, may be "natural," but it is also self-defeating.

The solution to the problem is as straightforward as in the previous case. Control your exposure to the antecedent events. *Simply don't stop.* Regain your balance. Relax. Let it flow. Slow down, perhaps, especially if you were out of control. But above all, flow into a couple more turns. If you are thinking you are tired at that point, go ahead and stop—*but not until you stop from a position of strength, a position of balance and control.*

SHAPING BETTER SKIING

There are as many different types of cues controlling skiers' habits and skiers' heads as there are skiers themselves. Although the process of active awareness is designed to pick out those cues which specifically affect your skiing, it is often difficult to change your exposure to them. For example, if you want to learn to ski powder, yet it precipitates destructive feelings and conversations with yourself, you are seemingly caught in a bind. Recall that all it takes is a few pairings of loss of balance and certain ski conditions to cause your avoidance responses to become almost reflexive. If you "go for it," scaring (or frustrating) the hell out of yourself in the process, you only add more fuel to the fire. On the other hand, if you avoid it, nothing new can be learned. Consider a dialogue we hear frequently:

> "I don't wanna ski over there, too much crud and bumps."
> "Aw, c'mon."
> "No. Why should I ski something I don't enjoy? I'll ski down this side . . . but I sure do wish I could ski that stuff. If I could, I'd ski it in a second."
> "Mmmmm, right."
> (Working way down easy side): "Well, I would, if only I could ski it."
> "Mmmmm, yeah."

All of that would be fine, of course, if it were not for the glaring discrepancy between your goals and your attempts to reach those goals. The occurrence of such discrepancies is a good indication that approaching the problem by *gradually altering the payoffs* will help considerably.

"Sneak up on it." That is the most economical way to describe shaping techniques. Shaping means successive approximations, taking a step at a time. In so doing, you are gradually changing your payoffs while at the same time you are changing the "value" of some of the contexts that cue your problems. Shaping is effective in both areas because it involves a relearning and reperceiving of the situation.

Managing Traversing Troubles

There are a number of avoidance behaviors that skiers share that could be rather easily modified by systematically taking things a step at a time. *The keys here are "systematically" and "a step at a time."* The classic example of this is the beginning or intermediate skier as he or she traverses back and forth across a hill, afraid to make that first turn down the fall line. All of the traversing in the world is not going to be an efficient way to learn to ski. Admittedly, it is a normal avoidance response—that is, a skiing habit you have taught yourself in order to avoid excess speed (nothing else seems to work at that stage) and imagined speed-related catastrophes (going face-first into a tree?). This explains its common occurrence. The problem is that it *does* become a habit, a kind of nonthinking behavior.

We could draw upon any number of illustrations of this, but the most extreme case was that of a young man who would ski *across* expert slopes, slow down (sometimes stop), and stiffly turn around to begin his next traverse across the hill. At least he was "skiing" the expert runs (and chopping up the run, much to the chagrin of the advanced skiers sharing the space with him). Most skiers with difficulty in speed control "find themselves" skiing across the hill in a manner far less exaggerated than this young man, but nevertheless progressing slowly if at all.

The application of shaping would work like this. Find a section of the hill that is *easy* for you. Visualize a path, perhaps fifteen feet wide at this point, going straight down the fall line. Ski it, making a few turns. What you are trying to do is change your psychology. You are beginning to shape a new skiing behavior. It is important that you start with a hill that is easy for you. Remember that you have learned the traversing problem because of your original reflexive response to loss of equilibrium. You have learned that traversing works to save you most, if not all, of the time. So you are stuck and not learning anything new. That is why it is essential that you begin shaping strategies with easy tasks. The last thing you want to do is relearn your avoidance responses or learn new ones. You do not want to stay tense or anxious—easily observable characteristics of "traversers."

Set your standards realistically at first. Achieving a realistic goal will enable you to tell yourself, "Well done, kid," and will be antagonistic to fear. You will be demonstrating to yourself that you *can* ski the hill without losing control. You can now do one of two things: you can either progressively narrow the "trail" so that you require yourself to make frequent turns, or you can move to a slightly steeper part of the mountain.

For the "low expert," the same strategy is useful. Picking a trail through the bumps and skiing it is a difficult task at first. The shaping approach to this problem requires the same gradualness and success experiences as for the beginner or intermediate skier. You might stay on the steeper, bumpy hill and get off two turns, then three, then four, and so forth. Alternatively, you might pick that trail through the bumps on a somewhat easier run and practice it consistently before you move on to something steeper. You will be learning to pick a trail and almost "photograph" it in your mind. And as you begin the run, if your first turn is good, the chance is greater that subsequent turns will be good.

Since none of this is particularly profound, it seems strange that there are so many persistent skiing problems. Though "shaping" is in fact a technical term for a type of psychological intervention that is used frequently with clinical populations, one hardly needs to be trained in psychology to understand and use it. The GLM method of ski instruction relies on it, for example, and has met with good results. Why, then, the persistence of so many of your personal embarrassments in the face of trying with so much effort to be rid of them?

The persistence of many problems is a result of failing to follow at least some approximation of these four guidelines for the use of shaping.

> 1. Be genuinely gradual. Take your time. If the problem is worth working on, we suspect you have had it for a while, so do not expect it to disappear at first try. You need some success experiences or you surely will give up the effort. Whether you are an outstanding skier or a beginner, many personal challenges remain for you. Understand that we are

not saying do not challenge yourself. We are saying don't *resensitize* yourself. (We will discuss this further in Chapter 14.)

2. Set your goals realistically. You could be gradual in the type of run you work on but unrealistic in the time you set to achieve your goal. As you are now aware, standard-setting is often a major psychological problem for skiers. You simply set yourself up for failure, predictably fail, and thus confirm your self-critical judgments.

3. Be consistent and systematic in your effort. This point is crucial. Suppose you attempt to shape new ski behaviors only on those days when you say to yourself, "Oh, yeah, I remember Chapter Six. I think I'll ski from the head down for a few runs and try that shaping stuff." Then you turn around and do it, quit for lunch, and return to banging down the hills in the way that is typically you. What price do you pay? You will resensitize yourself and you will stamp in your bad habits even further. And what are you saying to yourself at the same time? Are you angry with yourself? Are you disappointed that Chapter 6 did not work?

4. If you do not have the physical skills required, get some technique pointers from a certified instructor. Many times, however, our experience has been that skiers do know what is required and what they are doing incorrectly. They just can't seem to get it together. In that case, shaping tactics are exceptionally effective.

Skiing "Bad" Snow

Wet, fresh snow is a problem for many skiers. It becomes a problem for most skiers, in fact, when it gets chopped up. We have observed skier after skier avoid the sides of runs after fresh snow because it has been chopped up rather than skied down (as in the center of the run). We are not talking only about beginning skiers, either.

Shaping tactics are of use here. The question to be asked is: How might "bad" snow be approached within the guidelines thus far discussed? The logical answer may seem to be to stand in the bad snow, decide you will make just a few turns under control on a reasonably easy hill (you do not want to have to contend with speed control when you are just learning to manage the inconsistencies inherent in chopped-up snow), proceed with a few more linked turns, and then move up to progressively steeper hills. It does sound logical, but there is a better way.

In all cases of shaping, you must try to take advantage of skiing skills you already possess. It makes better sense to get your rhythm established where it is reasonably unchopped, and then to proceed into the chopped area for a few turns and then out again. Begin, perhaps, with one turn in and out. The criticisms we have heard of this strategy point out that it is harder to make the transition from relatively smooth skiing into irregular snow, so why make it more difficult? The observation is correct, but the conclusion is not. If you do an active-awareness analysis of the situation—that is, knowing the contexts—you will realize that the inconsistency (change) in the snow condition that almost throws you off is the same one that has triggered your avoidance on most occasions in the past! You never stay in it long enough to learn it. Perhaps you get thrown off balance in the transition, ski out of it, and stop with a few thoughts like "Whew, got to stay out of that stuff!" We have seen this happen again and again: you are teaching yourself the *difficulty* of that ski condition. Also, the transition into crud from smooth snow requires unpredictable changes in weight distribution and edge control, and it is exactly this skill that is required when you are in the middle of chopped snow, anyway. So start from a position of rhythm and stability, ski into the crud, and accomplish those things at once.

We remind you again: be systematic and consistent in your efforts.

LOW-PROBABILITY SKIING

If you have ever said to yourself, "I turn better right than left," you have had experience with low-probability ski behaviors—that is, behaviors that occur less frequently than you would like. All skiers share this problem. You turn better one way. You almost always initiate stopping to the side favoring your strong turn. You are practicing your strength, which doesn't need it, while ignoring your weakness, which does need practice. The payoff, of course, is avoidance of instability.

The psychology in this case is easy to change. After identifying low-probability ski behaviors—all of those circumstances in your skiing where you can say "I do it better this way than that"—systematically shape new ones. Let each occurrence be a cue to change your low-probability habits next time.

Here are a few examples of what we mean and some suggestions on how to "get more for your money."

Weak Turns

If you turn best to the right, give up your search for a right-handed mountain. Instead, start on the *right* side—that is, your *strong* side—of most runs. This forces you to turn left with the same frequency that you turn right—or suffer the consequences, like going into the trees. (Contrary to the opinion of one wag we know, turning left *is* easier than hitting the trees.) Doing this prevents you from slowly sneaking your way across the hill, toward your strong side, as you descend the mountain. Have you ever noticed how many skiers start on the side of a run corresponding to their weak side and end up on the opposite side? Sort of a sneaky downhill/traverse? They are not completing their turns to their weak side because it "feels more unstable." The payoff for emphasizing their strong side is the avoidance of that feeling of relative instability.

Weak Stops

Doubtless, you favor one side over the other for stopping. In other words, when you initiate a stop, you initiate to your strong side. Change that. Let each intention to stop become a cue for using your weak side. By "cue" we mean a reminder to yourself to stop to the other side. You will be surprised how quickly you can balance your stops.

"Path Pounding"

Change your psychology so as not to be a "path pounder." In other words, always try to take a totally fresh track down a run. If you did it down the center and loved it, great. Now use that psychological momentum to explore something new. On the next run, stay fifty feet to the left. On the run after that, try the right side of the trail. And so forth. Two benefits accrue. First, you get more variety of terrain (and experience) for your lift ticket. Second, if you had a bad run the first time, you've gotten away from the particular cues that were associated with it. If you have another bad run fifty feet away, it's still fine. At least you did not "stamp in" that one track. (Did you ever wonder why your skiing ended up in a rut?)

To sum up, use some active awareness to get in touch with whether or not you have low-probability quirks in your skiing. If so, let that circumstance be a cue to consciously choose and increase the low-probability behavior rather than avoid it. You will then be working on what needs practicing most.

REWARD NEW SKIING STRATEGIES

The major direct reward for skiing well is the feeling of balance, rhythm, and stability. Feeling your edges set. Using the moguls. Getting air and coming down well. Executing perfectly carved turns. These skills provide the joys, the exhilaration of skiing. They help quiet fear, anger, and self-criticism. The point is this: the reward for new skiing techniques is largely dependent upon whether the techniques work for you, not whether someone "rewards" you for them. "Working" is, of course, a personal definition that takes us right back to goal-setting. *If you set your goals unrealistically high, many strategies you attempt will be doomed to failure before you begin.*

Rewarding new skiing strategies is therefore a question of *rewarding yourself* for meeting personal challenges. As you consistently use shaping tactics to meet your goals, you will have a unique experience in skiing. If you are like many skiers, you will meet more challenges with more success than you have in any similar time span until now. You will be punishing yourself less, and you will be improving more. Most important, you will be enjoying *yourself* more as your own skiing companion.

And so Dexter slowed down. He decided to map out a shaping approach to solving his problems. He did know the technical skills required, and proceeded to take things one step at a time. On somewhat easier hills, he picked a trail and began skiing it, flowing with it. He stopped from a position of balance from time to time, and then continued. He moved to some steeper hills, still consistent and systematic in his use of shaping, and things began to flow together even more beautifully. He also realized he was now getting his money's worth for the price of a lift ticket.

No magic at all. Simply active awareness and consistency in his quest for smoothness, with the help of some operant learning principles.

EXERCISES

1. Recreate several instances in which you have avoided certain terrain or ski conditions. Now, note whether there were discrepancies between your avoidance responses and your "I-wish . . ." or "if-only . . ." comments. This recollection will be used to help identify areas you "wish" you could change but have not thus far worked on constructively.

2. Again recall your conscious decisions to avoid certain terrain or conditions. Do an active-awareness analysis of these: SENSE, KNOW, INQUIRE. Conclude the exercise by designing a realistic and gradual shaping approach to tackling the problem.

3. Itemize those times the mountain is *skiing you.*
   Do you stop at the crest of pitches, for example?
   Formulate a plan to change your exposure to those
   cues, using a shaping process.

CHAPTER 7

Relaxation: Antidote to Fear and Tension

The next time you go skiing, pick out the best skier you see on the mountain. Then pick out the most relaxed skier. Most of the time they will be the same person. Good skiing requires relaxation. Relaxation allows your skis to float in powder, absorb sharp bumps, and hold on ice without chattering. But skiing is not total relaxation. If there were not some tension in your muscles, you would fall down.

Actually, skiing involves a continual momentary tensing and relaxing of your muscles *in sequence*. Often, however, your muscles tense *against* one another in the reflexive tightening that comes from anxiety, perhaps "pulling you down" into a crouched position with your tail sticking out. The key to relaxing on skis is to let go of the tension in your muscles *before* you tighten them again. That is done in what amounts to an unconscious sequence. Then, opposing muscle groups do not fight one another.

Carolyn was an older, experienced skier. Her only problem was that with every turn she became increasingly tense. She would begin with an upright, relaxed body position, make a few turns, and be hunched over with her knees frozen in a three-quarter crouch position. Not only did every bump in the snow throw her off balance, but also her legs and back would become cramped after one or two runs and she would have to stop. Her problem was that she never relaxed her muscles *between* each turn. Rather, she would flex her knees, edge her skis, and stay in that position! For her, the key was to "let go" of her muscle tension between each turn and return to a more erect body position.

We have found that one of the commonest errors skiers make is to become frozen in one (usually crouched) body position. The solution is to unflex your muscles and let go of the tension between each turn. This letting go can be momentary, just enough to allow your body to return to a balanced posture. By letting go, you are preparing your muscles to tighten again. This allows you to make quick, strong turns instead of feeling as though you're cramped up and hanging on. After all, if your muscles are tense already, you can't tense them any further unless you cramp yourself up.

Speed is one of the factors in skiing that, for many people, trigger this "natural" tightening response. White knuckles on your ski poles, a common occurrence, freeze the rest of your body in a rigid position. It's as though you're trying to hang on. Pressing forward counteracts the force of speed against your body, lessening your need to want to hang on. Loosening your grip and dropping your hands allows the rest of your body to relax. Try this exercise and see what we mean.

> Sit on the front edge of your chair and hold your feet slightly off the ground. Imagine that you are accelerating over a few small bumps; bounce your feet up and down together. Do that first with your hands clenched and held up in front of you. Then do it with your grip relaxed, your hands by your sides, and your torso leaning slightly forward. Notice that your stomach, back, and hips are relaxed in the latter posture, whereas they were tense when you were "hanging on." The more relaxed posture allows your legs to be loose and to absorb any undulations in the snow.

That example supports the point that too much tension when you ski is counterproductive. The tension should be read as a signal to relax. Here are some other tension signals:

- when you feel your grip tighten on your poles
- when you become aware that your teeth are clenched
- when a bump seems to throw your whole body up or up and back
- when your head snaps forward but your body remains stiff as you go over a series of bumps
- when you notice that your legs are tired after one run, particularly on hard-pack

Each of the above signals should serve as a *cue* for you to relax every time you SENSE it is occurring. This is called "cue-controlled relaxation." Cue-controlled relaxation is how the relaxation skills you learn in this chapter should be used on the mountain. When you get to the bottom of a run and notice that you are "out of breath," you may have been skiing hard, but you may also have been holding your breath as you have been anxiously hanging on.

As the late Dr. Fritz Perls, founder of Gestalt therapy, pointed out, anxiety is the interruption of excitement by, for example, holding your breath or otherwise producing disabling tension. When you are anxious, you are very close to the excitement in skiing. Getting rid of that tension frees you to experience the excitement. So relax! The purpose of this chapter is to teach you that valuable skill.

MUSCLE RELAXATION

Relax? That sounds easy enough, but what happens when you try to do it? For most people, nothing happens. "I don't know what to do," they moan. Other people really *try.* All they do is get more tense. Paradoxically, there is nothing to do to relax. Relaxation occurs by *not trying.* Unfortunately, most people don't know how to "not try." The only times they do "not try" is when they are totally exhausted—as after a hard day of skiing, for example. Remember the last time you really skied your legs off? You probably felt so tired that you could hardly walk, and you thought to yourself, "I'm exhausted." You probably were, but you were also relaxed. Fortunately, you don't have to tire yourself out in order to "not try."

The way out of this trying paradox is to get some momentum going in the direction from tension to relaxation. Since you don't know how to "not try" to do this, you should first try something you do know how to do. Clearly, you know how to be tense. Simply tighten your muscles. For example, gently clench your teeth. Then stop. When you *let go* of the tension, relaxation occurs. That is because by clenching the muscles, you produce more tension than is common (or comfortable) for you, so it is easy to *let go* of some.

Identifying the Muscle Groups

Because there are many muscle groups in your body, you first need to identify them by tensing and relaxing them one at a time. (You can execute the following processes while sitting on a chair.)

> *Hands and arms.* Begin with the muscles in your hands and arms. To know which ones we are talking about, make a fist with your dominant hand as though you were gripping a ski pole, and cock your wrist away from your body. (For tennis players, this is the same way you would cock your wrist for a forehand stroke.) Tighten these muscles slightly. There is no need to strain the muscles. You need merely to be aware of the tension produced in your fingers and thumb, the back of your hand, and your forearm. Now, let go of the tension by unclenching those muscles. Do this as though you were suddenly dropping the ski pole or tennis racket from your hand. Notice that a slightly warm, pleasant feeling flows into your hand and forearm and that they feel slightly heavier. The next set of muscles are those in your upper arm, specifically your biceps. Tense these

by bending your arm at the elbow and curling your hand toward your shoulder. (This is the "Muscle Beach" pose.) To relax the muscles, drop your hand toward the floor. Notice the feeling of warmth that flows into these muscles and the heaviness that results.

Facial muscles. There are three groups of muscles in the face. The first is in the forehead and can be tensed by raising your eyebrows as high as you can so as to make horizontal frowns across your forehead. The second group is around your eyes and cheeks. Tense these by closing and squinting your eyes tightly. The third group is around your mouth and jaw. To tense these, clench your teeth and purse your lips as though you were a baby stubbornly refusing to be fed dinner. Tense and let go of each of these muscle groups separately so that you identify them and are aware of the contrast between feelings of tension and the warm, heavy feelings of relaxation that occur when you let go.

Neck. There are two separate muscle groups here. You can tense the first by bowing your head and trying to force your chin into your chest. Tensing the second group is achieved by pushing your head backward against the back of the chair, a wall, or any other object that will provide resistance.

Shoulders, chest, and upper back. You can tense the muscles in these areas all at once. Do this by taking a deep breath and holding it in your upper chest. At the same time, pull your shoulders back as though you were trying to bring your shoulder blades together. Notice that this creates tension in a band across your chest, around your shoulders, and across your upper back. When you let go of the tension in these muscles, allow your shoulders to slump forward as you let the air out of your lungs. Don't force the air out of your lungs; just let it go as you would with a deep sigh.

Stomach and lower back. You tense the muscles in your stomach by taking in half a breath and making your stomach hard, as though you were expecting someone to hit or slap you there. At the same time, arch your lower back forward, so that the small of your back is not touching the chair and you are sitting stiffly erect. Feel the tension—and let it go. Notice the contrast between tension and relaxation.

Hips and buttocks. Tighten the muscles in this area by clenching your buttocks tightly together and tilting your pelvis forward so that the small of your back is touching the back of the chair. Then let go.

Thighs. Clench the muscles in the front of your thighs by straightening your legs and holding your feet off the floor. Let go of these muscles by letting your feet drop down with a thud.

Calves. Point your toes downward to tighten your calf muscles. It is easy to cramp these muscles, so be careful not to tighten them too much. Let go of the tension and allow the pleasant feelings of relaxation to spread into your calves.

Shin. Along with your thighs, the shin muscles get the biggest workout when you ski. They are also the ones that are likely to be most tense after a day of skiing. (Or even before!) Tense these muscles by pulling your feet upward and pointing your toes toward your head, as though you were raising your ski tips just prior to getting off the chair lift. Then let go.

Feet. These are the muscles that may become cramped after a day of skiing if you have spent the whole day hanging on. When these muscles are tense, it is virtually impossible for you to get any flexibility in your ankles. You tense these muscles by curling your toes downward and arching your feet slightly, as though you were trying to hang onto the slope with your toenails. Tense these muscles, notice the tension, and let it go.

Relaxation Training

Once you have identified each muscle group and are able to tense it and let go of the tension, you are ready to begin relaxation training. First you need to find a setting that is conducive to relaxation, someplace where you will not be interrupted and where distracting noises are at a minimum. The best posture to use is one in which your body is partially reclining and is supported at the head, back, hips, legs, and feet. Reclining chairs are ideal but not essential. Stretching out on a couch or bed with your back and head slightly propped up will suffice. A comfortable easy chair and ottoman are also possibilities. Whatever furniture you use, you should be able to sit comfortably with your arms and legs uncrossed. The relaxation procedure works best with your eyes closed. However, until you are totally familiar with the sequence of the various muscle groups, you may want to keep your eyes open so that you can refer to this book or a separate list.

Once you are settled comfortably, you are ready to begin the tension-relaxation process. For each muscle group, we want you to *tense the muscles for five to seven seconds and then abruptly let go of all the tension* by letting your muscles go slack. While you are tensing the muscles, focus your attention on the feelings in that particular muscle group. When you relax the muscles, be aware of the pleasant contrast between the feelings of tension and relaxation. Focus your attention on the feelings of warmth and heaviness that spread through each muscle group when you relax it. Allow that warmth to spread over your body and soak into your muscles. You should focus on the relaxation part for thirty to forty seconds.

Initially, this process works best if you tense and relax each muscle group twice before moving on to the next group. If you find that any muscle group is particularly difficult to relax, you may tense and relax it a third or fourth time. During this process you may find that your mind wanders. That's O.K. If it does, simply focus your attention back on the feelings of tension and relaxation that you are creating in your body. Alternatively, you may find that you drift off so completely that you fall asleep, especially if you are doing this process at the end of the day. That's O.K., too. It's a sign that you are really letting go of the tension. If you find that you are repeatedly falling asleep during the relaxation process, however, you should try it at a different time of the day and/or change your posture so that you are sitting in a more erect position.

Let's review the whole training procedure:

1. Recline comfortably on a chair, couch, or bed with your arms and legs uncrossed.
2. Tense each muscle group from five to seven seconds, focusing on the sensations of tension in the muscles.
3. Abruptly let go of the tension and focus on the sensations of warmth, relaxation, and heaviness for thirty to forty seconds.
4. Repeat processes 2 and 3 with one muscle group before going on to another.
5. When you have completed the tension-relaxation process for each muscle group in your body, take a few minutes to remain seated comfortably and soak up the feelings of relaxation throughout your body before you go on to any other activity.

For the best results, you should repeat the relaxation process at least once a day for four or five days consecutively. As you become practiced, you will find that you can relax each muscle group with only one tension-relaxation cycle. Once you and your muscles become fully aware of the contrast in sensation between tension and relaxation, you will be able to let go of the tension in your muscles *without* tensing them at first. You will also find that you can relax entire areas of your body at once—that is, without tensing, you will be able to let go of all the muscles in your face, legs, or hands and arms.

Although you should practice this procedure in a private, quiet place, once it becomes "natural" you will find that you can voluntarily relax your muscles, genuinely "letting go," while working at your desk, driving your car, riding the chair lift, or on skis. To do this, you should focus your attention on the muscle groups in your body to check out the presence of any tension. Since with practice you will already know what it feels like to let go of the tension, simply let the feeling of relaxation occur. For example, if you are riding the chair lift and become aware that the muscles in your thighs are tense (perhaps as you contemplate your next run), shut your eyes, focus your awareness on your thigh muscles, and let go.

MENTAL RELAXATION

Tennis champion Yvonne Goolagong used to say that when she lost concentration during a match, her mind went "walk-around." A meandering mind can wreak havoc with your best intentions, whether in tennis, skiing, or something as "simple" as relaxation. You may find that as you do your muscle-relaxation exercises, your mind is thinking of your job, a new pair of skis, or a fantastic party next Saturday night. Although some of these may be pleasant to contemplate, they do not facilitate relaxation. In fact, they may even cause you to tense up with eager anticipation or worry. This is especially true if your mind is buzzing from a day of strenuous or exciting mental activity.

Many solutions have been proposed for this problem. One approach advocates turning off your mind. First of all, that's easier said than done for many people; and second, as we've said before, your mind is an asset not to be ignored. Instead of unplugging it, we have found that you can actually enhance your bodily and emotional relaxation by shifting your mental focus. Think of your mind as a receiving unit for a variety of electronic signals. Most of these signals activate you. They tighten you up with joy, excitement, anger, or anxiety. But a few of them calm you down. Those are the channels you need to select to enhance your relaxation. One of these channels is a visual one.

To experience this channel, go through your muscle-relaxation exercises until you are moderately relaxed. Then, with your eyes still closed, create an image in your mind of your *tranquil personal paradise.* This may be a deserted tropical beach, a tall, silent mountain high above the timberline, a calm, grassy meadow near a babbling brook, or a fur rug in front of a glowing cabin fire. As you continue to let go of the tension in your muscles, transport yourself to your tranquil paradise. Allow yourself to float into the scene and settle comfortably amid your surroundings. Let go more and more.

Whenever your mind wanders, switch the channel back to your paradise and sink into a state of relaxation.

Some people find that an auditory channel deepens relaxation. You might play a tape in your head of a peaceful strain of music. If you are able to keep this in your mind without effort, great. Use it to complement your visual scene. Many people, however, find that the focused repetition of a simple sound produces relaxation. With clients and skiers alike, we have found the use of a single word is effective.

Choose a one-syllable word that has a neutral meaning or one that denotes relaxation and *sounds* relaxing. A common neutral word is "one." Relaxing words are "calm," "warm," or "ease." Get into a comfortable posture and close your eyes. *As you exhale,* say your chosen word under your breath. At the same time, visualize the word (or the number "1"). When you inhale, don't focus on anything in particular; let your mind go wherever it chooses. As you exhale again, repeat the word to yourself. Repeat it with every exhaled breath for at least five minutes. Seven to ten minutes is even better.

Another method of producing mental relaxation is an inner spatial focus. This is useful for deepening relaxation you have already begun. To locate this channel you need merely to initiate the relaxation process through letting go in your muscles or repeating a monosyllabic word. *Then focus on the space between your eyes.* Concentrate your mental energy on that space. If your mind wanders, switch the channel back to that space. As you increase your use of this procedure, anxiety will seem "alien" and will become a *cue* for you to relax immediately. While riding the chair lift or the subway, you will be able to let go of tension by turning your attention to that space.

In the S.K.I. model of active awareness, sensing is an especially valuable tool here. As you gain experience in relaxation skills, you will be able to SENSE residual tension and *let it go.* As you gain experience combining your relaxation skills with your skiing, you will be able with increasing accuracy to make the distinction between normal skiing tension and anxiety-produced tension. You will be able to let the anxiety tension go almost reflexively every time you sense its presence. You have then reached an important goal: the "natural" use of cue-controlled relaxation as you are skiing.

EXERCISES

1. Practice the physical and mental relaxation exercises at home until you can "let go" without first tensing your muscles.
2. While reading, driving, or working at your desk, focus your awareness on your body. Let go of any extra tension that you notice. Do the same while riding the chair lift.
3. Practice momentarily letting go of the tension in your whole body between turns, especially in con-

ditions, such as bumps or ice, which usually cause you to tense up.

4. Use the feeling of speed on your skis as a signal (cue) to drop your hands, loosen your grip, press forward slightly, and relax.

CHAPTER 8

From a Hindrance to a Help: Changing Your Self-Talk

Recall the material in Chapter 3 on being your own worst enemy. If you are like a lot of skiers we know, you were having some conversations *with* yourself *about* yourself (and your skiing) as you read that material. Our experience has been that it hits most skiers right between the eyes.

The fact of the matter is, however, that you cannot just *stop* talking to yourself. You have been having these monologues since childhood. In fact, you may have observed that young children talk out loud to themselves while playing. That activity decreases as the child grows; the stream of conversation becomes internal, but it seems to continue unabated.

"Right," you say. "I'll just change my self-talk from fear or anger to 'constructive' advice." A sample:

> "I'm not going to be angry. I'll concentrate instead on what I should be doing. Don't be so stiff! Mogul threw me—don't sit back so far. C'mon, self, reach out with that pole. Don't let your arm get behind you like that. Pulls me back. Relax that leg. Don't face uphill!"

Sad to say, this tactic will not work, either. A stream of what-not-to-do's will set you up for a reemergence of the anger- (or fear-) talk. This chapter deals with what *to* do in order to change your self-talk from a hindrance to a help.

101

DIFFERENCES AMONG SKIERS

We have asked many skiers, at all levels of ability, what is going through their minds at various times on the mountain. We have found consistent differences among them, differences of both frequency and theme.

Advanced skiers and fast learners seem to have an *overall lower frequency* of destructive private monologues. Their self-talk is more of a help than a hindrance. They are challenging and coping more. Beginners, many intermediates, and slow learners seem to have an *overall higher frequency* of damaging monologues. Their self-talk is more of a hindrance than a help. But themes also vary.

Beginning and intermediate skiers seem to have more of a problem with fear-talk. Beginners are in a strange environment with strange new sensations. If you are a beginner, the feeling of long boards strapped to your feet, perversely waxed to make them go faster, seemingly wanting to slide out from under you, is strange indeed. Beginning/intermediate skiers are skiing new runs, perhaps wanting to push harder, but talking to themselves about the vagaries of moguls. Moguls, you may swear, actually reproduce themselves there in the light of day. Certainly they must in the dark of a moonless night.

With advanced intermediates and beginning experts, the self-talk tends to center on themes of frustration, anger, and impatience. Truly expert skiers also tend to get angry with themselves, but the destructive monologues occur with much lower frequency. They have learned to psych themselves up instead of out, seeing the run as a challenge, the bumps as exhilarating, setting personal goals, *feeling* their bodies and their skis. As an example, when we asked many expert skiers what they were thinking at the top of a very difficult run, we found it was almost invariably: "I'm picking out the best line down," "I'm challenging myself," "I can't wait." (Another common response was that they were "feeling" themselves skiing it, or "practicing in their mind"—the subject of Chapter 10, "Covert Rehearsal.") They were emphatically *not* thinking, "I wonder if I can do this" or "This run always kills me."

You have an idea of the category to which you belong. As you read this chapter, be actively aware of your own skiing monologues.

MASTERY VERSUS COPING

We can roughly distinguish two ways of dealing with problems: mastery and coping.

In the mastery model, your objective is to make the problem disappear. Theoretically, anxiety is reduced to zero; negative thoughts cease to exist; anger is completely supplanted by reasoned objectivity. You are supposed to master your work.

You have been brought up to believe that hard work will be justly rewarded. The "push-push-push" behavior so characteristic of Americans as we scurry about, "trying harder" to master our environment, is a response to our high expectations. Promotions. A's. Perfect kids. "As ye sow, so shall ye reap."

Well, it doesn't work for sex, and it doesn't work for skiing. It apparently works only for Avis. The problem with the push-push-push notion is that it invites an almost constant stream of self-criticism and tension, a preoccupation with the product rather than the process. Yet, like many other paradoxes in skiing, it, too, is "natural." Pushing has always been heavily reinforced in our society, and there is no reason to believe we skiers are less susceptible to social learning than other mortals.

The coping model, on the other hand, demands no miracles. Its emphasis is on process and progress rather than product. The product will come. You *will* flow, relax, float, ski in harmony with the terrain. But why batter down the front door when you can walk in the side entrance? (Dr. Don Meichenbaum of the University of Waterloo in Ontario has done a great deal of research in this area. Also, Dr. Albert Ellis, founder of Rational Emotive Therapy, has been among the pioneers in the clinical application of many of the areas discussed in this chapter.)

Learning does not happen instantly. You can enjoy progress a step at a time. It all depends upon whether you perceive through a "mastery" model, which demands perfection, or a "coping" model, which allows for progress. You crashed in the powder—or you fell laughingly in the fluff. You complain that there were five skiers ahead cutting up a trackless bowl, or delight that you were the sixth, rejoicing in a crystalline day. *The glass is half-empty, or the glass is half-full.* As the humanistic psychologist Clyde Reid puts it, "Celebrate the temporary." Relax, enjoy, experience the freshness in each new turn, the faces in the lift line, the sound of your skis, the squeak of the snow.

In the coping model, you can see that you have different standards and you *label* your experiences differently. Some residual apprehension is accepted as the thrill inherent in skiing. A little anger is O.K., as it serves to cue even further active awareness and relaxation.

It is probably impossible to eliminate judgmental and evaluative self-talk in skiing. Your body reflexively tenses when you almost "lose it." Your head reads that as "I must be afraid. My body is tense." That is the natural part of skiing and, of course, the reason your body is rather ineffectual at "teaching itself" to ski.

But in coping, you can *refocus.* To refocus is to view and interpret the problem in a slightly different way. It is the beginning of modification of your private monologues and relies heavily on using more accurate or appropriate interpretations of your skiing or ski conditions. In many cases, this amounts to "self-instructional training" of the sort in which you are instructing yourself to take things a step at a time, relax, and so forth. Here are a few examples:

(Watching an instructor and imitating poorly): "I'll never learn this!" The more accurate interpretation: "This is difficult at first, but it's coming."

(Expert skier falling in the bumps): "Dumb! You'd think I'd have learned by now!" The appropriate interpretation may be something like "Really had my rhythm. I just sat back too far."

(Advanced intermediate on a moderately steep run): "If I can't ski this by now, I ought to quit. Why can't I stay relaxed?" Alternatively: "Stop. Take a couple of deep breaths and relax. O.K., let's flow over these next several bumps. Good! That felt much better."

When we guide people in modifying their self-talk, they tend to have a united common reaction (out loud): "It is hard to believe this will help." And privately they say, "I can say it, but I don't think I believe it! It won't make me feel or do better."

Try to avoid the pitfall of talking yourself into a failure experience. The facts are these: first, you *do* generate a great deal of emotional arousal by talking to yourself; second, your physiology *does not* readily distinguish between internal and external input; and third, you *do* define yourself and your skiing by the way you talk to yourself about it.

YOUR S.E.L.F.

The full sequence of four steps necessary to change your private monologues from a hindrance to a help follows the acronym S.E.L.F. In practice, these flow together and are not so discrete.

1. STOP. Stop your thoughts of fear, anger, and catastrophizing. They have done you no good and will continue to be useless.
2. EVALUATE. Evaluate your standards. What do you really expect? Are you setting yourself up for failure as in the Self-defeating Syndrome?
3. LABEL. Label what happened realistically. Reinterpret in line with a coping model. This is also called "countering," by some psychologists.
4. FOLLOW UP. Follow up with reinforcing comments. Be good to yourself; compliment yourself for accepting and meeting your personal challenges.

S.E.L.F. MODIFICATION OF YOUR FEAR MONOLOGUES

Recall the equation: *risk minus fear equals peak experience.* If you are a skier with a fear problem, the chances are you recognize much of it to be self-generated. You are psyching yourself out (thinking how fearful you are), by letting the mountain psych you out (one example is stopping at the top of steep pitches). We acknowledge that risk is present, but if you are skiing, you apparently wish to take some risk. You now need to subtract the fear. (It is certainly possible to be *genuinely and realistically* fearful. If you have got into that situation once or twice while skiing, you are not unusual. Chapter 14, "When You Can't Do It," will be of interest to you.)

STOP your thoughts. There are several ways to do this. Distraction is one (for example, concentrate on the sound of your skis). What psychologists call "thought-stopping" is another. It works like this. First, get in touch with the contexts under which you begin your fear-talk. The common contexts are: after falling, while stopped above a steeper pitch, and when your body is already reflexively tense. Next, vividly imagine and recreate one of your fear-producing contexts. Establish the scene in your mind, feeling the anxiety, experiencing the context. Then abruptly slap your hands together, yelling "STOP!" (and we do mean yelling, right from the gut). This action will almost certainly stop your imagination and vivid feeling of the scene. Practice it several times with different scenes. Then begin to phase out the hand slapping and yelling and, instead, "yell" it under your breath. Practice this technique several times a day for perhaps a week.

You are now ready to use it on the mountain. When the fear monologues begin, yell "Stop!" in your mind. By so doing, you are initiating change in your self-talk by decreasing the perseverance of your catastrophizing. This is an essential first step, but it needs to be supplemented by the following.

EVALUATE your expectations. Almost simultaneously with thought-stopping, you should ask yourself, "What did I expect?" To seriously hurt yourself? What huge catastrophe?

You should be able to arrive at a clear definition of your fear. Expectations must change. It is not unusual for people never to have tried to *specify* an emotional upset. Of what *exactly* are you jealous? What *clearly* is the most disastrous thing that could happen? *Precisely* how will you hurt yourself? If you have not done this, do it now. You will need to develop this ability to the point where you can do it on the mountain. You may be surprised to find that when defined and carried to their logical conclusion, many fears are blatantly irrational. Others need more work.

LABEL. You have attached destructive labels to your tension ("I'm uptight"), to your falls ("Close call"), to the hill ("This is tough"), to the light ("I can't see the bumps. I'm going to crash for sure"), to the snow ("I can't ski this"), and so forth. If you do have a problem with apprehension when you ski, and are honest with yourself, you can sit where you are at this moment and recreate some of those monologues. The labels must change. You are psyching yourself out, *and your physiology knows it.*

The process of attaching more appropriate labels is often called "countering." Notice the sensible coping theme in these examples:

> "This light is tough, so I need to relax and feel more through my skis."
> "I almost fell, but my body tensing up is a cue to relax again now."
> "Well, everybody falls, and it isn't likely that I'll kill myself."
> "I can feel my muscles tensing. Normally, I would interpret this as fear. It's not, though. It's just a reflexive response, and I can feel myself relaxing again."

FOLLOW UP. It is clear that our social system neglects to train us to praise ourselves. The caricature of the person saying with shuffling feet, "Aw shucks, t'weren't nothin'," in response to genuine praise is not far from the truth. Now is the time to change that! You have stopped the catastrophizing, evaluated and rooted out some unrealistic fears, and labeled them more appropriately. Now, compliment yourself! You are moving toward your goals. Some examples of good FOLLOW-UP:

"Yeah! That helps me be more sensible."

"I'm not so tense right now—feels good."

"That old tension itself is beginning to be a cue to figure out what I'm saying to myself. I'm doing fine!"

"Hooray!"

Whatever. Your progress is personally yours. Enjoy and compliment yourself as the mountain begins to ski you less.

S.E.L.F. MODIFICATION OF YOUR ANGER AND FRUSTRATION

Sometimes you may get impatient with yourself for an obvious error. At other times you may get angry at your "psychology." It is interesting to observe this quirk in skiers: you may *know* that you are psyching yourself out in certain situations and then worsen the problem by getting terribly impatient with yourself for doing so! If you are not aware of techniques to change your psychology, your anger persists. Finally you arrive at the point where perhaps only half of the problem is caused by the original psych-out. The remainder of the problem results from the futility you experience as you "try harder" to resolve it. The point we want to make is that the S.E.L.F. modification of anger yields a double benefit. Change your original impatient self-talk a bit, and the rest follows beautifully.

STOP your thoughts. As with your fear monologues, the conversation has to stop. Use the thought-stopping technique to decrease the perseverance of your frustration and anger.

EVALUATE. Just what goal have you set for yourself that you are trying to reach with such pained futility? Especially with anger and impatience, evaluation and modification of your expectations are imperative—this goes back to the problem of setting yourself up to fail as you set your goals unrealistically high. You then fail, and there begin the "I told me so" recriminations.

"I will not get tense. I will flow over every bump, setting edges, carving turns, rarely falling. My legs will be like shock absorbers; my skis will carve perfectly; I will be a model of smooth control of anything the mountain has to offer today."

That was Pete, you may recall. The objective facts were that he could not, at that point, ski with that kind of grace. He was much in need of changing something!

LABEL. Here is how Pete got more sensible and relabeled.

"I can relax. Let me relax for a moment or two. O.K., for a couple hundred yards, stopping from a position of balance. There's my line. I'll absorb the bumps on this section."

There was an immediate change in Pete's skiing. He did not yet ski as a model of smooth control, of course. He needed some more technique pointers and more practice. But he skied at peace with himself, actively aware of his body and the terrain, freer of tension blocks. He was meeting a new challenge, and was now "ready," in the best sense of the word, for that further instruction.

Jill was experiencing the "expert blues." Normally a superb skier, she was, for some reason, having a series of bad days. She was complaining to her new skiing companion that she just did not normally ski this badly. But try as she might, she just could not show him her normal skiing. To make a long story short, it became apparent that she was skiing for him, judging herself against the standards she perceived him to have, tensely determined to get it together. A talk with him about her self-talk, plus some thought stopping, evaluation of expectations, and more appropriate labeling, "freed up" her head. Predictably, that one morning of active awareness and S.E.L.F. modification also freed up her skiing.

More than one skier has said to us, "O.K., if I change my standards for myself, where is the challenge?" Our response is that it is there, and more of a challenge than before. You eliminate the challenge only if you never attempt to *meet* your standards. Your standards are your own, not friends', not observers', not "I should's." The time to label more appropriately is when you are aware of self-critical responses to your skiing, aware of impatience, or aware of anger. At that point, these feelings are blocking your skiing. Letting them go is certainly a challenge. And working your way back up to your goal without battering your head against it is even more of a challenge.

FOLLOW UP. Needless to say, it is easy to compliment yourself when you are doing better. But since you are not used to complimenting simply "better," as opposed to "best," it is also easy to forget to do it. Please don't forget. Complimenting yourself increases the probability you will successfully use that helpful tactic again. It's good for you to be good to yourself for making improvements. And it feels great.

A DIGRESSION ON "VERBAL ECOLOGY"

We would like to make a comment about "verbal ecology" on the mountain. We have found that many skiers share our concern about it. When your anger or frustration monologues burst outward, remember that they are no longer monologues. They are potentially dialogues. Impatience with strangers or with your ski companion is as unpleasant for them as your anger is for you. Many times the unwitting recipient of the barrage makes the error of sympathizing. The sympathy, a "natural" response, is a nice payoff for you to stay angry and stay verbal about it. (We will deal with that further in Chapter 15, "Helping the Heads of Your Friends.")

But many times not a soul is interested in your self-flagellation. It is (to us) as paradoxical an experience to hear a stream of profanity on a beautiful mountain as it is to see cigarette smokers on the lift. The smoking is an oral privilege; the anger is an aural imposition. So if you have difficulty applying S.E.L.F. to your monologues, we have a hunch that many souls would appreciate your *not* telling the world about it. Think about that.

COPING COMMENTS

We would like to wind up this chapter with several more suggestions for appropriate coping statements. Some examples are evaluative, some involve labels, and some are positive follow-ups.

"Let's see—what is it I have to do to change my weight distribution in this wet snow?"

"Everybody falls. I can progress faster if I relax and realize that."

"My tension is a cue to stop and relax. I can feel myself relaxing more now."

"She has been skiing for years. I'll get there, too. Now, relax and watch."

"Just because they are psyched out is no reason for me to be psyched out. Don't prejudge the run."

"Those turns felt beautifully balanced!"

"I can learn this a step at a time if I quit picking myself apart. Let go of the tension."

EXERCISES

1. As outlined earlier, gain some experience with thought-stopping.
2. Creating your personal "counters" (labels) is essential. You can begin to do that off the mountain by setting aside five or ten minutes to sit back and relax. Recall and recapture the feelings during your recent bout with fear or frustration. Now, identify what you are/were saying to yourself and create several counters for each of those self-statements so you will be able to label differently. Write them down. Continue doing this as often as you can continue identifying different disruptive self-statements and a variety of counters.
3. As you are relaxing, recreate the above experiences. Feel them. Now *apply imaginally* the counters you just made up in the S.E.L.F. sequence. Remember that S.E.L.F. should flow to-

gether. Practice this as often as reasonably possible. Do it, for example, instead of daydreaming several times a day.

4. Apply your S.E.L.F. sequence *consistently and consciously* the next several times you are skiing. If you are consistent for several days, you will find that the S.E.L.F. sequence becomes "automatic." You will be redefining your skiing and yourself.

CHAPTER 9

Vicarious Learning: Extra Instruction at No Extra Cost

Mark, a college racer, put on his first pair of skis only four years before attending college. During high school he lived in an urban area far from snow, much less any skiing. Yet, in his first year at college he became the best technical skier on the team. After a year of seasoning with college competitions, he became a good racer who placed well in most races. Prior to his coaching in college, he had never had any formal instruction.

Have you ever wondered why some skiers improve so rapidly with so little instruction and practice? "Oh, they're just natural athletes," you say. O.K., but as we explained before, skiing is not a "natural" sport. It challenges our instincts for balance and self-preservation. Yet, some people are able to overcome all of these "natural" hazards and learn to ski relatively quickly. One of the authors says:

When I first saw Mark ski, I asked him how he had learned so quickly. I expected him to say that he had spent several winters in the mountains. Instead, he replied that he skied only on weekends. He'd made friends with some good skiers who took him with them to Mammoth Mountain. "Well, did they give you a lot of instruction?" I asked. "No, nothing much beyond what equipment to get and how to put it on. We were a quiet bunch, and we didn't talk much when we were together. They just skied, and I watched and did what they did." Taking Mark's experience with his friends as a key to how he learned best, I coached him primarily by having him follow me, first just in free-skiing and later in practice runs on racecourses. His progress was astonishing and gratifying. By the end of the year he was technically the best skier on the team.

Mark's rapid improvement is a classic demonstration of what psychologists call "vicarious learning," or "modeling." Modeling is not new to psychology or skiing. Psychologists have used this principle to help people overcome their paralyzing fear of snakes, heights, crowds, and public speaking. Ski instructors have also used this principle. When they say "Watch me!" and carve smooth turns down a steep slope, they are not doing it to show off. (Although there is some narcissistic gratification for all of us in knowing that people are watching us do something well—that is part of the joy of skiing.) The ski instructors are demonstrating the right technique for you. And modeling is one of the best ways to do it. Almost anything that can be learned directly can be learned vicariously. (That is, by watching someone else do it and then practicing it yourself.)

QUALIFIED MODELING

There is one major qualification concerning these statements. Vicarious learning is not useful in skiing if you are feeling anxious, angry, jealous, or depressed. It especially will not occur if, first, you are engaging in any self-destructive monologues, and second, the model is serving to trigger a fear-reaction in you. For vicarious learning to have a positive effect on your skiing, you need to be relaxed, alert, and at least neutral in your *self-talk*. So don't try to use the suggestions in this chapter if your number-one problem is fear or anger at yourself. If you do, the consequences are likely to be that you will fail to learn because your emotional state interferes, and you may conclude that you can't do it, that you're no good, and that you'll never be any better. If your primary problem is fear, or any other negative emotion, work on that first.

AVAILABILITY OF MODELS

Unfortunately, not all of your vicarious learning about skiing comes from ski instructors. Most of your ski time is not spent in ski school. So although the instructor has shown you the best technique, many other people on the mountain are showing you how to stiffen your downhill leg, stem every turn when you're trying to ski parallel, or bounce off the bumps when you should be absorbing them with your knees. The errors skiers make are far more obvious than the subtleties involved in truly fine skiing. They are also easier to identify with, since the response to loss of equilibrium is universal, natural, and well within the observer's experience. Weight distribution shifting slightly, subtle edge changes, independent leg action, a hint of tension here and relaxation there— all of these are much *more difficult to read* than a flailing pole, a stiffened body, or an edge left unset. Actually, you already "know" how to do many of the incorrect things. As we showed you earlier, your body will naturally do those things in the interest of self-preservation. What you learn vicariously from the poorer skiers is to be anxious and stiff when you should be relaxed and self-confident.

An example of this is the "stopping-at-the-edge-of-the-cliff" propensity that we discussed earlier. Recall the last time you had difficulty with the steep, icy part of a run. First, you stopped at the top of the worst pitch to peer over the edge. (Have you ever noticed that you can always tell that a difficult section of the trail lies ahead because there are a lot of skiers stopped at the top of it?) Wondering why everyone had stopped at the top, you watched a few others start down. To answer the question, you focused on the skiers who were having the most difficulty. Their skis were sliding rather than edging, their legs were locked in one position, their arms were stiff and awkward. In short, they looked petrified! While you watched, your body also began to stiffen. *You felt the way they looked.* That was vicarious learning. So when you pushed off down that pitch, you skied it with the same awkwardness they did, even though you are a much better skier!

You may also have observed some skiers who handled the difficult slope with ease. If you focused your head on them and imitated their fearlessness and good technique, congratulations. You used vicarious learning to your advantage. However, we have found that most people manage to cancel out the positive modeling provided by the better skiers on the mountain by saying something like "Gosh, they're good. I can't imagine skiing like that." If that's you talking, there goes your own worst enemy again. That is indeed unfortunate, for it is precisely your imagining you *can* ski like that which is the essence of vicarious learning.

You can make modeling work for you or against you. Either way, it will affect your skiing. This is especially true of your emotional responses. By observing relaxed skiers, you can facilitate relaxation; by observing skiers staying in the fall line, you can decrease your tendency to traverse too much. And by observing skiers who are having trouble, you can bring back all the fear and tension that you thought you had conquered in the previous chapters!

The Tense Model

At a national downhill training camp one winter, the coaches showed a film of a very difficult downhill racecourse the night before the actual race. The film showed racer after racer rocketing through a bumpy section of the course at 60 miles per hour, losing control and crashing into an explosion of arms, legs, and skis. The tension in the room became incredible. Any fear that had been conquered while practicing for the race was resurrected by the experience of watching the film. In the race the next day, those competitors who had used their heads to control their anxiety skied well. Those who hadn't were left to the same fate as the racers in the film. There were a lot of good skiers in the latter group.

That should be a lesson in itself. *Don't watch tense skiers.* The racers in the training camp should have attended to the skiers in the film who did not fall. Tense skiers have nothing useful to teach you. You don't need them to show you how steep the slope is, how hard the ice is, or how heavy the powder is. Your body will automatically—that is, reflexively—tell you if the terrain is frighteningly difficult for you. What you need to do is to let your body relax.

The Talking Model

Let's extend this point one step further. Remember how you can be your own worst enemy by making self-defeating statements to yourself? Your "friends" can be your "enemies" as well. Recall the last time you were skiing with a friend on a difficult slope. You were both trying to do your best, and you were actually handling it well, but your friend was really having trouble. She or he said, "Damn it all. This is really tough. I can't ski this stuff. I'm just not having any fun." The farther you skied, the more your friend complained. Our guess would be that you empathized with your friend. After all, you know what it's like to be having a bad day. So you agreed, "Yeah, this is tough stuff," and you began to ski less aggressively. Pretty soon, instead of your skiing the mountain, you discovered that it was skiing you. And you started to make the same self-statements as your friend: "Damn it all. I can't ski this stuff anymore. This isn't any fun."

The lesson here is simple: *don't listen to a skier who is having trouble.* If your friend is being his or her own worst enemy, don't let that person become your enemy, too. In Chapter 15 we discuss how to help the heads of your friends. To do that, you first need to be using your own head. So for now, just don't listen when other skiers complain. If necessary, ski alone for a while. The adage "Hear no evil, see no evil, speak no evil" makes a lot of sense when applied to your skiing! This does not mean that you should turn off all your senses when you ski. The emphasis in the adage is on "evil," meaning tension, fear, and self-defeating statements. We want you to use your powers of observation to your advantage, not to your detriment.

The Flashy Model

Since "looking hot" is a goal for many skiers, you may be tempted to choose the flashiest-looking skier on the mountain to imitate. Don't. What looks flashy may be the worst thing for your technique. Former Olympic champion Billy Kidd is one of the least flashy-*looking* skiers in the history of American ski racing. When he raced, he rarely looked fast to the untrained eye. Yet, he is one of the best. He doesn't look fast because he doesn't waste any motion. There is no excess baggage in his skiing.

On the other hand, there are a lot of flashy skiers with a lot of excess motion. When you learn vicariously, you imitate the most *obvious* elements. Unfortunately, in flashy skiers the most obvious elements are frequently the least essential.

PICKING YOUR MODEL AND LEARNING TO LOOK

To use vicarious learning to improve your technique (the physical aspects of your skiing), pick a smooth, steady skier to imitate. A smooth skier is modeling relaxation and balance, not speed or extraneous motion. Unless you are trying to learn to be a racer or a freestyle competitor, don't pick a racer or a hot-dogger. This is not to say that racers and freestylers are not good skiers. They are. It is just that they may not be the best models for what you want to achieve. A ski instructor is usually one of the best models you can find. Short of that, choose a friend who skis the way you would like to ski. *Watch* him or her. Just look. That sounds simple enough, but it isn't.

Most of us can't *just* look. We have to look with judgment. To demonstrate what we mean, recall the last time you watched a skier whom you wanted to emulate. What were you thinking? You probably thought something like, "That skier is terrific! I wish I could do that." You watched by judging. A better way to look is by experiencing what you are seeing. If the model is floating through loose powder, you feel your body floating. If the model is absorbing the moguls, you feel yourself absorbing the moguls. Practice just looking.

Turn on the television with the *sound off.* Simply observe, without comment, the actions of the people on the screen. Relax as completely as possible, letting go of tension, and then *experience* the movements of the people. Try picking out separate actions and feeling those if you find it difficult to simply watch at first. Then, put it back together. Let yourself experience the whole person, the whole action. Do so several times, or until you feel you are genuinely experiencing, without comment, your TV model. You should finally be able to *experience* all or just part of the model simply by tuning in without comment whenever you wish.

Once you know how to look, you should know what to look at. That all depends on those aspects of your skiing which you identified as needing change. Look at that aspect of the model which relates to your objective. The following are examples of things you may have slated for change and the corresponding aspect of the model that you should watch and experience vicariously.

Problem:	*Watch and experience:*
Moguls	Knees flexing and straightening
Weight too far back	Fanny; hands at end of turn
Powder	Up-and-down motion of whole body
Ice	Angle of knees into hill; edge control
Tightness	Knees; whole body flowing from turn to turn

If your problem is not so specific, watch and experience the model's entire action. Don't try to copy any particular aspect; just feel the whole process of the model's turns. Visualize the gestalt. Then imagine yourself actually experiencing the movement you are watching. Recreate that feeling when you ski.

WARMING UP WITH MODELING

Pretend you are at the mountain, about to begin a day of skiing. When you start your first run, what do you usually do? Most skiers think about which run would be the easiest warm-up run, the greatest challenge, or the least crowded. If you are aware of your body not being loose, you may do a few stretching exercises before you push off, but you probably don't do anything to get your head and body together.

One of the best exercises that we know for getting your head ready to ski is observing someone who skis well. Before you start your first run, perhaps while you are still on the lift, watch. All that you need is a good skier who is within view. As you watch, experience the sensations of that skier's movements. *Actually put yourself in that skier's body.* Before you push off on the first run, feel the movements that your model makes. We have found that doing this consistently at the beginning of the day on the mountain significantly decreases the time most skiers take to get their heads together.

THE CONTAGION OF JOY

Thus far, we have been talking about how to use modeling to learn physical technique. As you know, modeling also applies to your emotional learning. If other skiers *look* scared on a certain slope and you pay attention to them, you will feel scared. And you will ski scared down that same slope. On the other hand, you can also ski joyfully if you have a few joyful models around. There are several classic laboratory research studies that demonstrate this phenomenon, and it can be used to your advantage. (This section draws on the research of Dr. Albert Bandura on vicarious learning and Dr. Stanley Schachter and Dr. Jerome Singer on how and under what circumstances you label your emotions as a function of observing others.)

Laughter and joy are contagious. And so is courage. If one of your problems is that you become afraid, discouraged, or depressed, it is helpful to be around a person who is happy and unafraid. When you observe the model's joy or fearlessness, allow yourself to experience it. And be careful not to discount the model's emotions by telling yourself, "Well, she's only feeling good because she's skiing well. If I could ski like that, I'd feel great, too." The truth is that she's skiing well because of the way she's feeling.

Have you ever noticed a group of people who are skiing together and really enjoying themselves? It doesn't matter whether one of them is falling all over the place. The skier is still having a good time because he or she is participating in the joy of the group, "learning" the positive emotions of skiing through the company he or she keeps. The person is using the group to psych up, and it doesn't cost a penny extra. You can do the same.

There is one other place that vicarious learning of good skiing can occur: at the movies, especially *après*-ski in a bar! We're not just trying to promote ski movies in bars when we say that. Remember the anxiety that the downhill film produced in the ski racers? One of the reasons that this occurred was the *emotional atmosphere* in which the film was shown. Those racers were already experiencing a lot of prerace tension. Their race the next day was serious business. Contrast that situation with the typical *après*-ski atmosphere in a bar. People are relaxed and joyful. What better place to sit (or lie) back and observe films of powder or bump skiing? Under conditions of relaxation, your vicarious learning of the joyful, flowing aspects of skiing will be enhanced, especially if you make a conscious effort to *feel with* and get into the skin of the model. Let the atmosphere relax you, and let your imagination soar.

EXERCISE

The next time you go skiing, identify an aspect of your skiing that you would like to improve. It can be something physical like having looser knees or a more centered body position. Or it may be something emotional like feeling more joy or self-confidence. Be aware of the possible models to imitate. At first it may even help to do an active-awareness analysis of their skiing, as best you can. Once you have selected and observed a model (without judgment on your part), imagine yourself in the model's body and experience the sensations of his or her movement or emotion. Create that experience for yourself as you watch. Then take the experience with you when you start down the mountain.

CHAPTER 10

Covert Rehearsal: Head Work at Home and on the Mountain

There is research evidence showing that both men and women spend a significant amount of time on sexual fantasies. If you spent even a part of that time on ski fantasies, you would be amazed at the effect it would have on your skiing. That is what this chapter is about: working on your skiing by working *directly with* your head.

Psychological researchers have found that impressive modifications of both operant and emotional learning can result from what amounts to consciously guiding your fantasies. This process is often called "covert rehearsal" as it applies to voluntary behavior. "Desensitization" is a term referring to the use of fantasy in working with the reduction of fear. Both covert rehearsal and desensitization are a kind of mental practice. As you know, the separation of operant and emotional learning in skiing (and human behavior in general) is just about impossible. Several of the techniques that we present in this chapter primarily involve covert rehearsal; others primarily involve desensitization. However, the fact is that covert rehearsal probably also desensitizes, and desensitization also provides for some covert rehearsal. Both these techniques are among many of the covert strategies used regularly in psychotherapy.

Covert strategies have also been used extensively with skiers. Psychologist Dr. Richard Suinn of Colorado State University has been coaching the U.S. Olympic Ski Team in certain psychological tactics for several seasons. His reports in the scientific literature have been encouraging. He calls his technique visuo-motor behavior rehearsal (VMBR). It is basically covert rehearsal in that racers are asked to relax, visualize the course, and rehearse running the course in their minds. This is approximately the same technique that Billy Kidd employed in the 1970 World Championships when he was unable to ski the practice runs as he normally did owing to an injury. Dr. Michael Mahoney reports its use with gymnasts. It even extends to basketball: a 1967 study in the psychological literature found that by mental practice alone, people were able to increase the number of baskets they shot from the free-throw line.

Besides the fact that it works, one of the strongest arguments favoring the use of covert rehearsal is that it can be employed anywhere. To make it work, you need to sit back and *clear your mind* of the day's distractions, *relax,* and *visualize* your skiing, *sensing* your feelings.

LEARNING COVERT REHEARSAL

Try some covert rehearsal. We will guide your fantasy, for the moment.

Sit back and relax. To covertly rehearse a run, begin by visualizing the hill. Some people find it easier to visualize themselves skiing up to it and then looking at it for a moment. Others begin by viewing themselves on a lift looking over at the run. Experiment with whatever is the most effective aid to vivid visualization.

Next, imagine yourself looking down the run, picking the line you wish to take. Recreate that scene as clearly as possible. It may take a little practice if you are not typically a visual daydreamer. Include the sounds, the sights—anything that captures reality for you.

Finally, imagine yourself pushing off. See your skis moving over the snow. Feel your knees absorbing any bumps. Fantasize the sounds and recreate the ski experience as completely as possible.

The point that follows requires that you try the above rehearsal sequence *before* reading on. Otherwise, the point will be lost. Take a moment to do that now. . . .

Fine. Exactly what were you *seeing?* Think about that for a moment, recreating the scene if necessary. Describe what you were seeing. Did you see yourself skiing from the perspective of an outside observer? Dreaming frequently happens that way—you *see* yourself from the outside. Did you observe and comment on "you" just as another skier might?

Here is an alternative. When we asked you to recreate the ski experience as completely as possible, did you imagine yourself *within your skin?* In other words, was your view through your own eyes? In that case, were you *feeling* your body, the terrain, your skis? Were you even, perhaps, aware of what your head was doing?

It is worth practicing the ability to get *inside your skin* as you covertly rehearse your skiing. See the terrain passing by, feel your feet, your legs, your arms, and the wind in your face. Listen to your skis and to the snow. If you have difficulty doing this, some of the active-awareness exercises in Chapter 4 may be useful to help you increase your ability to visualize.

KNOWING WHAT TO FEEL

If you are a beginner and do not know what to feel, you have an obvious problem. Beginning skiers have not had the success experiences of intermediate and advanced skiers. It is all too easy to unknowingly covertly rehearse the wrong skills, and the tactic will then be working against you. If you are a beginner, the most powerful use of covert rehearsal will be to rehearse (and practice) *relaxation* on skis. A little later, as you acquire some success experiences and *know* the feeling of a proper edge set (or whatever), you may be ready to include those skiing skills in your rehearsal sequences. At all points, it is very important that you do not feel high levels of fear.

For an intermediate skier, knowing what to feel is much less of a problem. Presumably, you have had some success experiences, and your skiing will benefit greatly from some covert rehearsal of those experiences. Again, you should not experience high levels of fear.

Among experts, covert rehearsal is one of the most useful psychological tactics available, as demonstrated by Dr. Richard Suinn's work with competitors in the 1976 Winter Olympics. Dr. Suinn was the first on-site psychologist the United States had ever provided for its team.

ON-THE-MOUNTAIN GUIDED FANTASY

There is one time while you are skiing that proper covert rehearsal is invaluable. Recall our discussion of the Stoppers in Chapter 6. If you are a Stopper, when you "lose it" or go out of control, you stop with a "Whew!" and think about the "close call." Or perhaps you stop with frustration and begin your self-critical anger.

We pointed out that you should *always* slow down or recover before you stop. You then stop from a position of strength and balance. At that point, *before you continue,* covertly rehearse the next part of the run. Stop other thoughts, shut your eyes, pause, and rehearse. Be sure you are rehearsing a skiing *sequence* and not just an isolated behavior. For example, you don't want only to rehearse a knee-bend over that bump over there, even if bending your knees is your problem. You want to rehearse a skiing *sequence* that leads up to and includes several knee-bends. Do that for several moments at every opportunity. Let stopping become a cue that now is the time for your guided fantasy. Incorporate the sounds of the skis around you into your imagery. *Feel* what you realistically intend to do on the next part of the run. You are now accomplishing so much at once (thought-stopping, relaxation, coping imagery, and covert rehearsal) that the benefits are exceptional!

Expert skiers use covert rehearsal almost all of the time, often "unconsciously." They are picking a "line," "mapping" the run. This comes with practice—you learn to "read" the mountain. Included in the "reading" process is the covert rehearsal of skiing that line. Gaining experience with covert rehearsal is what makes "reading" the mountain second nature to the expert.

OFF-THE-MOUNTAIN GUIDED FANTASY

The same techniques can be used at home, riding to the area, on the lift, or during boring conferences at work. Make a boring moment useful! It is an ideal time to practice your guided fantasy. You can enhance it by incorporating your immediate environment into your fantasy. A breeze becomes the wind in your face. A pencil becomes a pole. Your shoes become your boots. (A friend of ours claims she incorporates so much that the background sound of a typewriter becomes her chattering teeth. We suspect that goes a bit far.)

A young friend of ours, an excellent ballet skier and aspiring all-around freestylist, was bringing home some rather poor grades. His parents were justifiably proud of his skiing, but perturbed about his academic performance. His teachers felt the same way. They inquired whether the young man was "daydreaming" about skiing. Sure enough he was, but what they considered "daydreaming" was his guided fantasy. He was covertly rehearsing his art. Although the grade issue remains unresolved, his freestyle is improving dramatically!

Covert rehearsal is a chance to use your mind in a most constructive and satisfying way. Take advantage of it!

FEAR AND FANTASY: DESENSITIZATION

Learning to relax your muscles and your brain may be all you need to overcome the tension that is a "natural" consequence of learning to ski and moving up to steeper runs. You may be able to apply it nicely, along with other tactics, while on the mountain. However, for some skiers, this is not enough. You may have developed a seriously disruptive fear response to specific aspects of skiing. You are quite tense *before* you encounter the thing(s) you fear.

The rest of this chapter deals with that problem. If you do not find certain aspects of skiing chronically fear-producing, you may wish to skip to the next chapter. If, on the other hand, your fear goes beyond some normal "tension," and you have been unable to handle it with the techniques thus far discussed —for example, control of antecedents, self-talk, relaxation on the mountain—this material will be extremely valuable to you. Frankly, it does involve some concentrated and conscientious effort on your part. But if your fear problem is chronic, and you are committed to coping with it, it will be well worth it to you.

As we discussed in Chapter 4, part of developing active awareness involves inquiring about the context of your ski problems. Since one of your problems while skiing is that you become tense or afraid, you are probably aware that this occurs in some contexts more than others. Some people get increasingly tense as the slope gets steeper, the bumps get bigger, or the hill gets icier. For others, flat light or deep powder produces tension.

If you could change those contexts, you could overcome the psychological problems with your skiing. But other than changing your *exposure* to some of your antecedents (as discussed in Chapter 6), you cannot do much to change most of the contexts themselves. Now, left with no option but changing his or her *exposure* to problem contexts, the typical skier with a serious fear problem chooses to avoid them entirely. Alternatively, the skier tries them while so tense that he or she cannot possibly ski well (the skier then gets angry and frustrated—and *stays* fearful, to boot). New terrain remains untried. New skills remain undeveloped. But that need not remain the case.

Fortunately, it *is* possible to change the fear-producing *qualities* of that nemesis of yours (bumps? the steep? speed?). To change the fear-producing *quality* of your contexts, you need to *desensitize* yourself to them.

In order to desensitize yourself to contexts that produce fear and tension, you need to start with something that is not too scary, cope with it—that is, relax with it—and move up one step at a time. This is like the graduated approach we explained in Chapter 6 in the section on "Shaping Better Skiing." In this case, however, it is a covert rehearsal process. Instead of being done on the mountain, it is done entirely with images.

This is all desensitization is—*the imagination,* accompanied by minimal anxiety, *of a graduated sequence of fear-producing scenes.* As you can see, it is essentially a type of covert rehearsal, but for several technical reasons is thought to work somewhat differently. Of all the psychological techniques discussed in this book, desensitization has received the most attention (and support) in the research literature. It is basically a three-step process: learning relaxation, formation of a hierarchy, and desensitization proper.

Learning Relaxation

First, you learn to relax. We assume you have done that. *If not, go back to Chapter 7, "Relaxation," and put this section down for a week or two.* We mean that. If you have a really serious fear problem, a two-week pause to learn to relax is a must. It is a minimal investment, and in desensitization it is an *essential* first step.

Formation of a Hierarchy

Second, you form a desensitization hierarchy: the graduated sequence of scenes we mentioned above.

To form a desensitization hierarchy, first identify the context in which your fear occurs. There may be more than one context. (If so, there can be more than one hierarchy, one for each context.) Now evolve a list of items (situations) that belong in your hierarchy. When you have identified the context for your fear and tension, think of the situation that is *most* tension- or fear-producing. This will be the top (most difficult) item in your hierarchy. Then think of the situation that is *least* tension- or fear-producing in the same context. This will be the bottom (easiest) item in your hierarchy. Now think of all the other situations that could be part of the context. You will find it easiest to write each situation (scene) on a 3×5 card so you can shuffle them around. Now rank them from most to least tension- or fear-producing. The list, which should contain about eight to twelve items, approximately evenly spaced as to the degree of anxiety each causes, is your hierarchy.

Sound confusing? Don't be worried (and don't get tense) if you are puzzled. Below is a sample hierarchy. Use it as a model for your own hierarchy (or hierarchies).

Paul's problem: anxiety, tension
Context: steep slopes
Hierarchy (from most difficult to easiest):
1. Making the first turn over the crest of the steepest part of a crowded narrow "most difficult" (black-diamond) trail.
2. Standing at the top of a narrow "most difficult" (black-diamond) trail that is crowded.
3. Standing at the top of the same trail with only one other skier on it.
4. Standing at the top of the same trail with no other skiers on it.
5. Looking at a crowded, narrow "most difficult" trail from the chair lift and wondering if I dare go down it.
6. Looking at an empty, wide "most difficult" trail from the chair lift and wondering if I dare go down it.
7. Skiing down a "most difficult" trail once I have made a few turns and gotten my rhythm started.
8. Standing at the top of a narrow "more difficult" (blue-square) trail.
9. Skiing down the same trail once I have gotten rhythm started.

As you can see, Paul discovered that the elements of this context that cause him the most fear and tension are steepness, narrowness, crowds, and getting started down the trail. Paul could have included several more items in the middle of the hierarchy. The criterion you should use for adding more items is whether the step from experiencing any one item to the next would produce a big jump in fear, anxiety, or tension. For example, if Paul felt that experiencing the step from items 6 to 7 created a lot of anxiety, he could have included an intermediate one such as "Skiing down a 'most difficult' trail that I know gets less steep, the farther down I get."

The same approach, graduated scenes decreasing in their tension-producing aspects, would be used for a problem with speed on uneven terrain. The lowest hierarchy item would be a little speed on smooth terrain, and the highest would be rather high speed on rough terrain.

As you can see, the principle is the same for the design of all hierarchies, but its apparent simplicity should not seduce you into being careless in designing your own. It is an important step.

Desensitization Proper

Once you have identified the context of your tensions, developed a hierarchy, and learned to relax, you are ready to put it all together in the process called desensitization. This consists of pairing your relaxation with the context that historically produced your tension. (Remember that it was the pairing of your *tension* and the context that caused the problem in the first place? You are now going to "neutralize" the ability of the context to elicit tension.)

The purpose behind this process is to allow yourself to experience vividly the items in your fear hierarchy without becoming tense. Start with the least-fear-producing item on your list, then move up to the next most difficult item in the hierarchy. By this process, you are "whittling away" at your fears without ever letting any tension build up around them. The process works because you have broken your fears down into manageable components. The steps are as follows:

1. Relax your mind and body, using the procedures in the first two sections of this chapter.
2. Vividly picture the context of your *lowest* hierarchy item. (It is best to do this in a reclining position with your eyes closed.)
3. If you experienced *any* tension or anxiety while

imagining yourself in the context of that item, *immediately* stop imagining that scene and switch your attention to the "tranquil paradise" scene to facilitate your physical and mental relaxation. Repeat the auditory cues—for example, "calm," and so on—and allow yourself to become relaxed again.

4. Switch your attention back to the fear-hierarchy item and vividly imagine yourself in that context.
5. If you experience any tension, repeat step 3.
6. When you can imagine yourself in the context of the hierarchy item for about thirty seconds *without* feeling tense, switch to the next higher item.
7. Repeat these steps for each item in your fear hierarchy at a rate of no more than three per day. If you get stuck on one and can't seem to stay relaxed when you are imagining it, you have taken too large a jump in your hierarchy. Make up one or two intermediate items (as with Paul's hierarchy above), so that each step is manageable.

The two most important aspects of the desensitization process are a vivid experience of each scene and an immediate escape from the scene if it makes you feel tense. If you find that you are going through your hierarchy without experiencing any anxiety but you still feel tense when you think about the fear-producing context, you may not be imagining the scenes vividly enough. Take some extra time to practice your imagery.

Begin by allowing yourself to become relaxed in a reclining position. With your eyes closed, imagine yourself reclining exactly where you are. Visualize the room. Be aware of the smells, sounds, and textures that surround you. Then switch your imagination to any scene that you experience every day. (This may be your desk at work, supper at your dining table, or a daily commute through traffic.) Visualize that scene and experience all the sights, sounds, smells, and textures that are part of it. Repeat this process with several more familiar experiences. When you can vividly duplicate these experiences in your imagination, you have sharpened your imagery enough for the desensitization process.

Once you have imaginally experienced all the items in your hierarchy without feeling tense, you are ready to experience them in reality *(in vivo)*. The process is the same except that instead of imagining yourself doing something, you actually do it. If you begin to feel tense, stop doing it and use some physical ("letting-go") and mental relaxation (images, word cues) to become relaxed again. Supplement these with positive self-talk. *Just as with the imaginal process, it is important to work on the items in the hierarchy one at a time.* This is basically the shaping approach discussed in Chapter 6. For example, in Paul's hierarchy he avoided looking at, standing above, or skiing down any black-diamond trails until he stood above and skied down the easier (blue-square) trails without feeling tense. When he became tense, he stopped, closed his eyes, and practiced his relaxation before proceeding.

By so doing, Paul alleviated his inordinate fear and was coping nicely with contexts that formerly disrupted his skiing. With that taken care of, and when he used some S.E.L.F. tactics and covert rehearsal besides, his skiing took a real spurt.

A couple of closing comments. Desensitization is a process that requires you to be conscientious in your undertaking. It takes more systematic planning and more regular sessions than perhaps any tactic in this book. But it is an extremely useful one if you are chronically fearful and yet wish to ski.

If it does not seem to work for you, there are several things you must check:

- Are your goals realistic? You are not trying to fearlessly bash down the supersteep without the technical know-how, are you? If you are, you are in a situation that is realistically fear producing. Good luck.

· Are you fully relaxed? Have you practiced relaxation for a couple of weeks, at least five or six times a week? In our culture, relaxation skills will come in handy all of the time and are well worth the twenty to thirty minutes' practice per day.

· Are you imagining vividly? Can you sit and recreate and experience the tension? Especially if you imagine your most-fear-producing scene? If not, you will need further practice with your imagery. (Another method with which you may wish to experiment is to have a friend quietly read to you your hierarchy scenes from the 3×5 cards, describing and embellishing them as you find most effective. Have your friend terminate the scene when you signal that you feel anxious, exactly as in the instructions given earlier.)

· Are you moving through the hierarchy too quickly? Or proceeding to the next scene before you feel relaxed about the present one? Create some intermediate scenes if necessary.

· Remember to do your hierarchy *in vivo* in that cold, crisp mountain air. On your first day on skis during or after completing the hierarchy, *work up to* the most-fear-producing situation you have thus far completed *but not beyond.* Be sure to continue to use your relaxation skills on the mountain as you are doing that.

· Supplement with covert rehearsal and appropriate modification of your self-talk.

EXERCISES

1. Practice developing your imagery daily. Shut your eyes from time to time, imagining your surroundings. Move up to increasingly remote scenes.
2. When your imagery is good (it may already be),

practice your covert rehearsal of skiing whenever possible. Once or twice a day at home, plus using covert rehearsal on the mountain, will be enormously beneficial.

CHAPTER 11

Concentration:
Metaphors and Rhythm

One of the biggest problems in skiing, whether in competition or for recreation, is a lack of *concentration*. And one of the biggest obstacles to concentration is your thinking. A wandering mind can trip you up more easily than a patch of ice, a clump of wet snow, or an abrupt mogul. One of the authors remembers that vividly.

Several seasons ago, I competed in an annual spring skiing race. Although the race was strictly for fun, it employed the same dual slalom elimination format that the professionals use on their circuit. After qualifying trials and elimination heats, I reached the finals. Concentrating on every turn, I was skiing well and felt confident. The first run of the finals was no different. I won by almost half a second. On the second run, I skied the upper part of the course well and pulled ahead by a couple of ski lengths. At that point I thought, "I'm ahead, I'll win." Instantly, I caught my ski in a rut and shot off course. My opponent sailed by to an easy victory. Seven and a half runs of perfect concentration, punctuated by one distracting thought, turned victory into defeat.

The next season, I entered the same race and again reached the finals. My technique was good. My only worry at that point was my concentration. Last year's mental lapse was a sharp memory. The difference was that I used a technique I had been developing for recreational skiing over the past few years. I geared myself to a certain rhythm and locked myself into that feeling by playing a piece of surging music in my head before the start to clear my mind of all thoughts. I won both runs comfortably. When I finished the second run, I was aware only of the rhythm. Victory was nothing compared to the experience of total concentration.

METAPHORS

Concentration in skiing requires an integration of mind and body. This means that your head has to experience the sensations of your body. To do that, you need to be able to translate your body's sensations into mental images. The best medium for that is the metaphor. Metaphors are not new to psychology. Sigmund Freud and Carl Jung used them to perceive the experiences of their patients' minds. Metaphors are even more common in the arts. Poets, painters, and composers use them to recapture mental and physical experiences or to create new ones. As psychologists, we have borrowed from the arts to develop metaphors that translate the physical aspects of skiing into mental images so that your mind can experience what your body should be doing.

You are already familiar with the use of visual images of other skiers to facilitate learning. Observing (Chapter 9) and covertly rehearsing (Chapter 10) ski techniques are powerful processes. You can enhance the power of these images by developing a few metaphors that go beyond the physical realities of your body.

A BODY MADE FOR SKIING

For many skiers, especially beginners, putting on skis is like beginning life all over again. Walking is out, skiing is in. Being hobbled by heavy boots fastened to cumbersome planks can be a humiliating experience for a body used to moving by putting one foot in front of the other. Instead of having feet that represent approximately 12 to 15 percent of our height, the body that we take skiing has feet as long as we are, giving us the shape of an inverted "T." What we need are some metaphors to adjust our minds to this new body. One of the most useful is to experience your feet operating the way they need to with skis on. The following process is designed for that purpose.

Sit straight in a chair with your feet flat on the floor and parallel to each other. They don't need to be touching, but they shouldn't be more than nine inches apart. Imagine that your feet are *one* car and on the floor in front of you is an S-shaped highway. Your toes are the front wheels of your car. Your objective is to *steer* your toes along the curves of the highway as it passes beneath your feet. Remember that your feet must work in unison. At first look at your feet as you do this. Then close your eyes and *feel* yourself steer your feet in unison. Do this for two or three minutes. Add some hills and valleys in the road. Follow these with your feet, picking them up off the floor as necessary.

Now imagine that your feet have grown and your toes are actually six inches beyond the ends of your feet. Continue to steer them over the curving, hilly highway for another minute or two. Really feel your toes out there.

Now imagine that your toes are twelve inches out in front of the ends of your feet. Keep steering them. When you are comfortable with your toes way out there, extend them another twenty-four inches. Really sense what it is like to have control over your toes three feet out from your body! Continue to steer them up, over, around that curving, hilly road for another minute or two.

If you ask people what makes a ski turn, they are apt to say, "The side camber," "No, the edges," "No, the flex of the ski." These answers are not really correct. Steering your feet and twisting your knees makes your skis turn. The preceding exercise gets you to experience *steering* your *feet* instead of trying to turn your skis.

It also gets you to experience your feet as being as long as your skis, making your skis an extension of your body. You should practice this metaphor daily for about five minutes until you can really experience what it is like to have your toes in the tips of your skis. When you go skiing, carry that experience with you. Practice it on the chair lift by closing your eyes and steering your "toes" (ski tips) over the imaginary curving highway passing below you. When you are actually skiing, continue this metaphor on a smoothly packed slope that is not too steep. As you experience it, you will be concentrating on your skiing. In fact, when you are really *experiencing,* the concentration is automatic.

A Friendly Environment

Unless you ski every day, the habits of skiing probably will not become "natural." This means that whenever you go skiing you are entering a foreign environment, one that requires you to act in "alien" ways. A large part of the "alienation" in skiing is a result of the way you construe this ski environment. Except for those experts who view all conditions on all trails and all mountains as a beckoning challenge, all skiers encounter conditions that they regard more as a threat than a challenge. For many skiers, large moguls and deep powder are two of the most "dangerous" conditions in skiing. Yet they can be the most friendly, offering a multitude of peak experiences. For this to occur, the skier needs be open to their "friendliness." Metaphors can facilitate this attitude.

Bumps. When confronted with a slope of big moguls, what do you usually see? One friend of ours visualizes a "field of tank traps." Another sees "huge teeth, waiting to grind me up." Neither of these images is very conducive to a friendly relationship with the mountain. On the other hand, you can also view the bumps as a giant staircase built for your graceful descent. Instead of being a tank trap, each mogul provides a platform for your turn, making the slope less steep. Visualizing the bumps in this way allows you to *use* them to your advantage rather than be intimidated by them (which produces anxiety, tension, and avoidance).

If you are fighting the bumps, the *action* of skiing moguls can also be difficult. Some skiers feel that when they go over bumps, the mountain is like a bronco trying to buck them off their skis. A more friendly metaphor is to think of the action of the bumps as *caressing* your skis and massaging your legs. Because they are friendly touches, you want to caress them back by moving your skis *lightly* over their crests, almost like waves. If viewed this way, skiing bumps becomes an action of retracting your knees to allow the bump to pass beneath you.

Powder. Skiing in powder, whether it is six inches deep or sixty, is like entering another universe. It can produce either an incredible "high" or a miserable depression. You can feel as though you are floating or drowning.

We use the water image here intentionally. The best metaphor that we have for skiing powder is being in water. Most people have difficulty with powder because they fight it. They feel "unnatural" *in* the snow because they are used to skiing *on* it. Trying to ski on top of powder snow is like trying to swim on top of the water. If you fight it, you will sink. But if you let yourself be *in* it, you will find that it supports you. Once you stop fighting powder snow, you will notice that it requires less effort than skiing on hard-pack, especially if it's steep.

Powder is a *floating* experience. Although the technique is obviously different, the sensation is like bodysurfing. You need to let yourself be in the snow and let it support and carry you just as you are supported and carried by water. If you don't struggle against it, the snow will begin to buoy your skis as you accelerate, just as water buoys your body.

The next time you venture off into the deep, approach it with the same interest and enthusiasm with which you approach swimming. This is not to say that there is nothing more to powder skiing than being in water. Powder-skiing *technique* is best learned from an instructor. The metaphor is designed for your head to let your body get in there and learn, instead of fighting the snow.

Your Own Metaphors

A word of caution. Some of these metaphors may not work for you, and you will be tempted to say, "That's crazy! Metaphors don't help skiing." We want you to know that these metaphors work for us and other skiers we know. If they don't work for you, the problem is not with the idea of metaphors, nor is it with you. Rather, it is with *these* metaphors. If they don't work for you, we want you to discover your own mental images—metaphors that *do* work for you. When you are experiencing a metaphor that you can relate to, your mind will be experiencing your body's sensations. That's concentration. That is also SENSING.

Ski instructors have helped people find metaphors that work by sharing their own images with their students, but you can discover them, too. Recall the perfect day of skiing that you recreated in the exercise following Chapter 4. As you reexperience that day (or any other time that you had a good turn, a good run, or a good day, or you handled a difficult condition for the first time), notice what your mind is experiencing. If you are really into the experience, you may notice that images appear. You may feel yourself drifting underwater or soaring above the earth. Or you may be experiencing something unrelated to skiing or physical activity at all. Whatever images you experience are your metaphors. They are the ways your mind experiences the sensations of your body. By recalling and reexperiencing those images when you're *not* skiing, you are preparing your mind and your body for when you *are.*

RHYTHM

Have you ever watched a freestyle ski competition? For the ballet event, the competitors select a piece of music to accompany their performance, just as in figure skating or gymnastic floor exercises. Music and rhythm are integral aspects of human movement. They are also part of the peak experiences in skiing. Music psychs up your emotions, and rhythm coordinates your movements.

Many skiers have discovered this for themselves. They hum their favorite melody as they glide along a gentle ski run. But when they get to a difficult section of the trail, *the music stops.* And the fear-talk often takes over. In composing the musical *The King and I*, Rodgers and Hammerstein showed that they understood a lot more about human consciousness than most skiers when they wrote "Whistle a Happy Tune." The lyric describes the use of a rhythmic melody for coping with a fear-arousing situation.

Music seems to block out thoughts about fear. This may be because of the complementary nature of the right and left sides of the brain. Dr. Robert Ornstein and others hold the opinion that we *alternate* between functions of the right and left brain instead of using them simultaneously. Thus, it may be that when you are experiencing right-brain phenomena (like rhythm and music), there is less likelihood that left-brain phenomena (like angry or fearful self-talk) will interfere with your skiing. In other words, concentration on a right-brain activity like experiencing skiing appears to be more compatible with another right-brain activity (music) than with a left-brain activity (linear thinking). You should be aware that these explanations are hypotheses, not scientific facts. However, the phenomenon is real: rhythm improves concentration. *And the more difficult the terrain, the more you need rhythm and concentration.*

The Beat of Different Drummers

Anne is an advanced intermediate skier who typically made graceful linked turns down the slope—until she got to a steep pitch. There she would stop, traverse, sideslip, make one turn, traverse some more, and get psyched out, despite her ability to ski directly down any pitch the mountain had to offer. The problem was not in her technique; it was in her rhythm, or lack of it. Her instructor suggested to her that she was not turning frequently enough. He suggested that he follow her and instruct her to turn whenever he thought she should. As soon as she started down the next steep pitch he said, "Turn." Immediately after she completed her first turn, he said again,

"Turn," and repeated "Turn, turn, turn" behind her down the slope. When she reached the bottom, she was euphoric. For the first time, she had skied directly down the fall line of a steep slope, and had done it masterfully. On the next run, he suggested that she instruct herself by saying "Turn, turn, turn, turn" aloud at frequent regular intervals. She did so with equally pleasant results. On the following run, she repeated the word to herself and skied the fall line with new confidence.

The instructions to turn were not the significant factor here. Anne already knew how and when to turn. The problem was that her anxiety about steep slopes had blocked her rhythm. By listening and then saying the regular *sound* of the word "turn," she was establishing a rhythm for both her mind and her body. The rhythm for her body enabled her to make linked fall-line turns. The rhythm for her mind maintained her concentration and prevented her left brain from interfering with experience-destroying thoughts.

We want to emphasize the importance of this last point. It is difficult, if not impossible, to *turn off* the thinking part of your brain. Your brain is working full-time unless you are unconscious. Rather than disconnect your brain from your experience, we suggest that you integrate the two by consciously providing rhythmic and metaphoric experiences for your mind.

Concentration can be maintained by any rhythmic experience. We have two friends who are fantastic big-bump skiers. They sound like a pair of steam engines as they blast down through a field of moguls. Their "Choo!" coincides with the initiation of every turn. Some skiers, including a lot of racers, use this noisy expulsion of air to force themselves to breathe as they ski. Although it is also useful for that purpose, our friends admit that they do it to maintain their rhythm and concentration. Their "Choo" achieves for them what Anne's "Turn" does for her.

Dancing Together

One other way of establishing rhythm is to pick up the beat of another skier, especially in difficult terrain. It has been our experience that the "follow-me" approach models a *rhythm* as much as it does a particular ski technique. There is only one caveat in this process: contrary to what many skiers would have you believe, there are many different rhythms to skiing. If you happen to follow a model whose rhythm is different from yours, you destroy your own timing and flow. Instead of improving, you get worse. Those of you who have experienced the frustration of skiing behind a model who is outside your rhythm know what we mean. For those of you who haven't, it is like trying to waltz with someone who is doing the fox-trot. Occasionally the consequences are worse than just stepping on someone else's toes. If you follow directly behind someone, his or her rhythm becomes an unavoidable part of the gestalt. You're stuck with it for those turns whether it fits or not.

The only way to discover whether you and someone else have the same tempo is to "dance" together. Try to follow that person's modeling. You will know if it doesn't fit because you will feel more awkward with each run. If that happens, don't force it. You can still benefit from the other person's modeling. Stand still and observe, experience, and imitate. You will also know if the "follow-me" approach does fit. You will find yourself flowing with the other person. *Without your thinking,* your movements will parallel the model's. You will *feel* it.

Whatever your own source of rhythm, we encourage you to include it in your skiing. Some people have found that the counterpoint of baroque music makes a nice accompaniment to their bump skiing. We have a friend who takes Strauss waltzes with her whenever she skis powder. Another friend plays rock music in his head for blasting through the crud. Everyone skis to the beat of a different drummer. It does not matter whether you play an elaborate symphony in your head or merely repeat a single sound; the important point is that you *facilitate your concentration* with rhythm. When you are doing this, you need not turn to the exact beat of the music. When and where you turn depends on the terrain as much as it does on your intention and your music. In fact, there are some situations, like the racing example at the beginning of this chapter, in which you would not want to play music while you were actually skiing. Music is a vehicle for getting in tune (literally) with the mountain. It gears your mind for a rhythmic experience.

EXERCISE

Whenever you encounter something difficult, you need your rhythm the most. Start your music before you start making your first turn. Get your rhythm going first. You will find that after one or two turns of your rhythm, you will pick up the rhythm of the mountain. Incorporate the "music" of the sound of your skis into the movement of your body and your awareness of the snow.

CHAPTER 12

Falling and How to Use It

All of the awkwardness in skiing, all of the bad "survival" habits, and all of the tension, both reflexive and voluntary, are intended to do one thing: to keep you from falling. And why not? There are many reasons to try to avoid falling. Let's take a look at some of them:

- You might get hurt.
- You might get wet or cold.
- You might hurt someone else.
- Other people might think you're not very good.
- You might think you're not very good.
- You might feel embarrassed.
- Your inner ear and autonomic nervous system resist your not being upright.
- You might lose time.
- Your friends might get tired of waiting for you.
- Your mother told you not to do anything undignified.

All of these (except for the last) are good reasons for not falling. (They are also good reasons for not going skiing.) The best way to be certain you don't fall is to stay home. On the other hand, if you go skiing, you are going to fall. The two are inseparable. Like it or not, gravity, which causes you to fall down, also pulls you down the mountain as you ski.

Actually, skiing begins with a fall. In order to start your skis down the slope, you cause your upper body and hips to fall forward. However, you avoid landing on your body by bringing your skis along with you. A fall occurs when your feet and skis move at a different rate or in a different direction from the rest of your body. So the best way to keep yourself from falling is to keep your feet and skis under you. Another expression for having your feet under you is "having balance."

Essentially, skiing is *"balanced* falling." This becomes obvious if you watch downhill skiers like the Austrian champion Franz Klammer. His gold medal run in the 1976 Olympic downhill was a beautiful example of staying within the boundaries of balance while "falling" down the course at an incredible rate of speed. Although he appeared to be out of control to many observers, he was in almost complete balance as he used gravity to produce the ultimate in speed.

It's our guess that you don't consider *"balanced* falling" to be a problem. In fact, you'd probably like a little more balance in your falling. We are making this point to stress the importance of falling in skiing. Most skiers think that skiing is the opposite of falling; to do the former you should avoid the latter. When you try not to fall, what happens? You fall, of course. Or you regress to gentler slopes that provide no challenge, no risk, and no peak experiences. And that's not really skiing.

There are basically four causes of falling. The first two concern physics. One of them is gravity, and you can't change that. The second is "faulty" balance. (Though this problem is outside the scope of our book, there are many ways to improve your balance. One of the best is to practice gymnastics.)

The other two major causes of falling are psychological. One is too much tension. If you are reading this book from front to back, you already know how and why tension affects your skiing and what to do about it. The fourth cause of falling is too much relaxation. This is characteristic of skiers who, on the way to the ski slope, send their brain out for a beer, leaving themselves mindless for the rest of the day. Although these skiers rarely get hurt, they fall a lot, usually more than the tense ones. Unfortunately, they don't learn much from their falls. (How can they? Their learning apparatus is down in the bar.) On the other hand, they are having so much fun that they probably don't mind (literally). If you are this type of skier, we are happy to leave you to your falls. The last thing we want to do is interfere with someone else's fun.

Tension, however, is a different story. Tense falls are psychologically unpleasant and physically riskier. The tension triggered at a fall, although it is reflexive and natural, gets in the way of improvement. If you can minimize some of the tension, each fall will become a valuable learning experience. That is a good goal to work toward.

FALLING AND TENSION

Most beginning and intermediate skiers *are* tense when they fall, and with "good reasons." Since we think falling is O.K. and can even be beneficial, let's take a look at these "good reasons" as well as some ideas for changing the labels in your S.E.L.F. modification.

1. Fear of getting hurt. This is always a possibility in skiing. That's part of what makes it a risk sport. The best protections against this are, first, good safety bindings, adjusted by a knowledgeable binding mechanic in a ski shop or ski department, and second, the confidence to say no when you can't do it (see Chapter 14). The odds of getting hurt under those two conditions are negligible. Knowing this can help you fall without fear, and you are therefore forced to have fun with, and learn something from, your falls.
2. Fear of getting cold and wet. You can reasonably worry about this only if you are not wearing adequate clothing. Money invested in good ski clothing is money well spent.
3. Fear that you might hurt someone else. You can avoid this more easily by skiing under control than by not falling. This means not going closer to another skier than fifteen feet and stopping *below* skiers standing in the trail.

4. Fear that other people may think you are not very good. Only someone who's never skied before will think that a fall represents "bad" skiing. All skiers fall. If anyone is going to judge you by your skiing, he or she will base that judgment on the way you ski when you're standing up, not on the way you look falling down.

5. Fear that you might think you're not very good. Same answer as number 4.

6. You might feel embarrassed. Number 4 again. If you really feel that falling is something to be embarrassed about, you haven't realized that *all* skiers fall. Furthermore, as Gestalt therapists have said, "Being embarrassed is getting caught at something you like."

7. Fear that your autonomic nervous system doesn't like being upside down. So what? You overcame your resistance to falling down and learned to walk, didn't you? Besides, the snow is a lot nicer to fall on than the kitchen floor.

8. Fear that you might lose time. Where's the fire? Unless you're in a race, you're not going to miss anything by falling down a few times. If you are in a race, your objective is to go as fast as you can without falling. That means that you're trying to be right on the edge of falling, and sometimes you miss. But that's part of the sport of ski racing. You wouldn't be there if you weren't willing to take the risk of falling.

9. Fear that your friends might tire of waiting for you. Don't laugh at this one. We know quite a few skiers who are very sensitive about holding up their friends. If you're one of them, you might want to check it out by asking them. If it really bothers you, you have two choices: you can choose to ski by yourself or with someone else who is slower-paced, or you can tell your friends to go on ahead and you'll either catch up or meet them in the lift line.

10. Fear that your mother might disapprove. If you're serious about this one, there is not much we can do for you without an appointment.

FALLING FOR FUN

Remember how much fun it was as a child to throw yourself into a snowbank or tumble down a hill of sand or jump into a pile of leaves? There is real joy in throwing yourself off balance intentionally and knowing that you're going to land safely. Consider diving into a swimming pool. You actually fall in under control because your upper body moves ahead of your feet. Falling is fun so long as you are not afraid of the "catastrophes" that we addressed in the previous section—or of any others that you create in your mind.

To be able to enjoy falling in skiing, you must work up to it. The basic principle underlying working up to falling is the same as that underlying working up to anything you fear: do it one step at a time (see Chapter 6). The following is an exercise to help you decrease your tension and increase your comfort with falling.

First of all, you must know where to fall. There are two locations you should take into account: one is the place on the mountain; the other is the place on your body. For your first intentional fall, pick a place on the slope where there are no rocks, stumps, trees, or ice, and preferably one with a slight grade. Pick a place on your body where you have some padding. With skis off, sit down in the snow. Before you get too comfortable, get up and do it again. Get up and do it a third time. You have just taken three falls. Nothing to write home about, but not bad for starters. Now roll a little when you fall, adding some motion. Put your skis on and repeat the falls.

Now for a moving fall, beginning with skis off. Make sure you do this on a slope with a moderate grade and soft-packed snow. Start by running and rolling. Do that a few times. Then put your skis on. With your skis on, your fall should be just like a baseball player's feet-first slide into second base. While moving, hold your poles up out of the way, sit down on your hips and back, and keep your feet up so your skis don't catch in the snow as you slide. Repeat this several times until you can do it without tension. *You are doing it without tension when you are truly loose enough to sit down like a puppet whose strings have been cut.* Practice until you get to that point.

Now SENSE how you are feeling. Intense? Silly? Awkward? Joyful? *Are you having any fun?* If not, you are still too attached to being upright, and you are taking yourself too seriously. Remember how much fun you had playing in the snow as a kid? Adopt that metaphor and repeat the exercises from a six-year-old viewpoint. Let yourself get to know the snow. Roll in it, taste it, smell it, feel it. It won't bite, and it won't let you down when you fall.

If snow is not available and you want to practice falling anyway, you can repeat these exercises on a bed, a pile of pillows, or soft grass. If you're outside, wearing your boots and poles can make the experience even more real. It will also make it easier for you to laugh at yourself.

Why are we encouraging you to enjoy falling? Obviously, we don't recommend it as the preferred way to stop. And we're not suggesting that you *try* to fall. We just want you not to get hung up about falling. Being able to enjoy falling is important for several reasons. First of all, if you can realize that falling is fun and is a natural part of skiing, you won't be so apt to punish yourself when you do fall. Second, by giving yourself permission to fall and enjoy it, you free yourself *not* to fall so much.

Finally, of course, the tension is not blocking you anymore.

FALLING FROM THE HEAD DOWN

Thus far, we have suggested exercises for your body in falling. We also have a few things for you to do with your head. First of all, if you're so tense about falling that you can't attempt the exercises in the previous section or you find that they don't loosen you up, you probably need a more formal desensitization to the fear of falling. Refer to the desensitization discussion in Chapter 10 if that is the case, and go back to work on a hierarchy around falling. As part of the desensitization process, rehearse the mental image of yourself falling and not getting hurt, while still being as loose as a rag doll. Hold that metaphor after completing desensitization; relax into a graduated sequence of falls on the mountain when you actually practice falling.

After the Fall

The above material is designed to prepare your head *for* falling. How about *after* falling? We know some skiers who immediately stand up, look around to see if anyone noticed, and brush themselves off until there isn't a flake of snow left on their bodies. These are the people who haven't gotten over "good reason" number 6, embarrassment. We know other skiers who react to falling by beating the snow with their ski poles while cursing the conditions, their equipment, and themselves. These people are stuck in "good reason" number 5— they take their falling as a personal reflection on their ability to ski.

Others review in their minds how close they came to really getting hurt ("good reason" number 1), thereby traumatizing themselves for the rest of the day. Still others leap to their feet and ski off down the mountain without so much as cleaning the snow off their goggles, as though they were late catching a plane ("good reason" number 8).

None of these reactions permits the skier to experience the fall. As a result, nothing is learned, and tension is increased. He or she either avoids the experience by pretending it never happened or distorts it into a physical near-catastrophe or a severe blow to the ego. These reactions are all examples of how *not* to fall from the head down. On the other hand, we have some suggestions for how to *use* your head after you fall.

Adopt the mental set of being *interested* in your fall. Before you get up, take a look at how you got there. Review in your mind what happened. What were you thinking, feeling, and doing just before you fell? Were you focused on the sensations in your body and the terrain immediately in front of you, or was your mind all over the place? If concentration was an issue, consider one of our metaphors or create one of your own to keep your attention. How did your body fall? That is, what happened physically to your body? Pay attention to whether you always fall the same way. Is there a pattern to your falling? If so, you may need to make only a minor correction in what you're thinking or doing.

Finally, pay attention to what you're saying to yourself after the fall. Are you being critical of yourself or something else? No one and nothing is at fault. *You just fell, that's all.* If you must attach labels to your fall, consider it along positive rather than negative lines. Was it spectacular? Was it the sort of fall that would make a good opening for ABC's "Wide World of Sports"? Was there anything to laugh about? Circus clowns and slapstick comedians make a living out of falling for laughs. Did you make anyone laugh? Most important, did you make yourself laugh? There is a lot of humor in falling. When you fall, keep that image in your head.

EXERCISES

1. Review all your "good reasons" for not falling. Take the point of view that they are *resistances* to experiencing falling and give yourself permission to fall.
2. Practice falling in the graduated way we described. Repeat this until you can be relaxed about falling.
3. If you have so much tension about falling that

practicing does not work for you, set up a formal desensitization process. (See Chapter 10, "Covert Rehearsal.")

For unplanned falls:

4. Relax. Note whether you are doing a "whew-that-was-close" monologue. If so, stop it.
5. Relax. Review how you got there to see if you've learned anything about what to correct in the future.
6. Relax. Hold the image of a playful child in your head and allow yourself to experience the humor in your fall.

CHAPTER 13

When You Think You Can't Do It: "Bad Days"

If you believe you cannot do a particular run, or if you have defined your day as a "bad day," you will be so tight that your skiing will suffer. That mountain is as you perceive it to be. And that mountain certainly looks different on "bad days."

John paused briefly at the top of one of the most challenging runs on Aspen Mountain. He fantasized he could almost *taste* the hill. He picked a line, took off, in love with the risk, the fantastic high, his body moving with grace and a resilience approaching perfection. . . .

Bruce paused briefly at the top of one of the most challenging runs on Aspen Mountain. He knew he should be able to do it and, with reservations, tried to follow an extraordinary skier through the bumps. He felt terrible and was doing poorly as muscle groups strained against one another with reflexive responses born of apprehension. . . .

Same mountain, nearly the same line through the bumps. Seconds apart in time, but different skiers with very different heads. Let's look at that for a moment.

John *knew* he could do it. Bruce thought he *should* do it. The run was not really inappropriate for Bruce. He was not a polished expert by any stretch of the imagination, but he was a good skier, having had flashes of brilliant skiing over the past season or two. So he knew he should be able to do it; he had the skill buried away somewhere in his *nervous* system. He *nervously* thought he would give it a try, but he was not really a believer. (Notice the pun and you notice the problem.)

WHEN YOU THINK . . .

Faith is amazing. The process of just believing in something is enough to alter your physiology and your perceptions with startling results. In skiing, if you *believe* you will have trouble with your skiing on a particular day or a particular run, you can bet you will.

So you think you can't do it. Why might you *believe* that? For one thing, when you are learning to ski, that reflexive tension is there. As the typical skier progresses to more difficult hills, some of that reflexive tension remains. Some skiers seem to get over it more easily than others. Or at least some skiers are able to put the tension in proper perspective, perhaps as part of the risk/thrill that is much of the exhilaration inherent in the sport. The skier who does not put the tension in proper perspective, the skier who does not see the run as a challenge but rather as a threat, is going to be catastrophizing and wondering if he or she can do it. The wondering ceases when the tension and associated flailing about on the hill is read as *evidence* that he or she could not do it. ("See, I told me so!") The wondering ceases, *and the believing begins.* As you can see, that is a variety of self-talk. The self-talk is being maintained because it fits, and then becomes your picture of yourself.

That is the nitty-gritty of what defines a "bad day"! Unquestionably, every one of us has had a bad day. It usually begins with a bad run or two. Perhaps the snow or your skis do not feel quite right. Perhaps there is some residual tension from getting a later start or from personal thoughts. Perhaps even some residual booze. All you need, for whatever subtle reason, is a couple of bad runs *plus* the acceptance of your skiing as *evidence* that you must be having a bad day.

Thus the cycle begins: every problem adds further evidence. More tension. More problems. More evidence. There is a clear discrepancy between the way you think you *should* be skiing and the way you are in fact skiing. The mind of a skier having a bad day is a potpourri of cognitive refuse.

. . . YOU CAN'T DO IT

We have found that many skiers do not know what they mean when they say they "can't do it." It's the problem of active awareness again. Even disregarding the apprehension and/or disappointment in your skiing for the moment, how is it possible to make the changes you wish if you do not have a specific, realistic definition of what needs changing?

Start by asking yourself a couple of questions when you experience the "can't-do-it" feeling. Are you skiing for yourself, your friends, or (worse yet) strangers? We hope you are challenging yourself *for* yourself. Imagine, for a moment, looking your worst as you are skiing that run. So what? Imagine falling. So what? Your friends may think, "Ouch!" and yell, "You O.K.?" Strangers may simply think, "Ouch!" Skiing *for* other people, always seeking the compliment, is a futile and nonconstructive undertaking. Thus, if you are tensely thinking you can't do it for them, you are being neither reasonable nor rational. Give yourself a firm admonition to *stop it,* and replace the thought with a more personal challenge.

Your personal challenge needs to be reasonable and realistic. Especially on bad days, you need to essentially start over. Here we remind you of the problems with standard-setting that we share. Competition and high performance standards are strongly reinforced by our culture. You need to work out of that trap: if your standards are unrealistic, you will obviously fail to meet them. If they are unrealistic along with having a bad day or thinking you can't do it, you have just given yourself more excellent and accurate evidence that you can't! We ask you again: Can't do what? When you think you "can't do" a hill or when you have defined yourself as having a bad day, stop immediately and ask what you are expecting of yourself.

There is one other point we want to make about thinking

you can't do it. The most probable way for you to believe you *can* do it is to have a few successful experiences. So set your goals at an achievable level. There is nothing like reinforcement to make a believer out of you.

BUT BE HONEST WITH YOURSELF

You must develop a sensitivity to whether or not you *think* you can't do it or really have reached your limits. Otherwise, you will not be challenging yourself sufficiently to learn. You will be saying no out of habit instead of discovering the broad new possibilities you can open up by *using* your psychology in skiing from the head down. Accordingly, recall and reconstruct a few earlier experiences and get in touch with how you responded to them. Your limits were (or will be) reached when, *in spite of using the procedures in this book:*

- Your fear is genuinely disruptive in that you can't cope with it.
- You have never skied a hill this steep, and you are falling constantly—that is, far, far out of proportion with the usual.
- You cannot change self-critical thinking (and acting).
- You are yelling and/or otherwise sharing your misery with your wife/husband/ski companions.

CHAPTER 14

When You Can't Do It

If you're given a choice, the answer when you can't do it is short and sweet: *don't!* Here is why.

Skiing from the head down is based upon psychological tactics to help you *de*sensitize yourself to destructive inner and outer contexts. The relaxation strategies, the self-talk material, shaping your skiing, developing skills in covert rehearsal—all of these are used to turn the laws of human learning to your advantage. You end up a far better skier and a far better companion (for yourself as well as for others).

It does not take a great deal to *re*sensitize yourself to the ski conditions and terrain that bothered you before. To resensitize is to relearn many of your involuntary emotional responses and have them interact with and influence your operant learning (see Chapter 2). It is far too easy to get talked into skiing a hill that will precipitate feelings of fear or anger. Unless skiing from the head down is a habit for you, your interpretation of your feelings and your skiing *will* resensitize you.

A suggestion for some control of antecedents is appropriate here. Do not allow yourself to get talked into something too difficult, something that will cue a great deal of fear. But some active awareness is also appropriate. Do not just talk yourself out of a challenge when you may need to be challenging yourself. Consider whether, even with the use of skiing-from-the-head-down tactics, the risk-minus-fear equation *does* equal a

peak experience. If it does not, you are resensitizing and setting yourself back. Avoiding resensitizing means sometimes
saying no.

SAYING NO WITH GRACE

Saying no to skiing companions who ski from the head
down is not a problem. Just say no. It will be perfectly understood. They could justifiably ask you to do a little active awareness and discover you are saying no because you have carefully
thought it out or because you are getting sloppy with your
psychology. It is hoped you will already have done this before
you have said no. In any case, if you do not wish to take that
run, say *no* and *don't* take it. Both you and your companions
will be comfortable with that.

But suppose your friends have not read this book. Their
urgings are likely to make you feel like a kid being called
"chicken" in front of the person you most want to impress. And
yet you have thought it out and opted not to ski that run.

People typically say no by holding someone or something
else responsible. They make statements using "you" and "it"
instead of "I." Here might be a typical dialogue with an incon-
siderate ski companion.

> "Let's go over to Bellygrabber Pitch."
> "Nope. You go. It's not fun."
> "Aw, c'mon. It's fun and it's easy enough."
> "It's not easy." (Thinking: "It's terrible. Quit pushing me.")
> (Determined): "You can do it. I've seen you do the same
> kind of hill. I'll go slow, for chrissake."
> "It's no fun. Go ski the damn thing if you want to. You're
> always trying to push me."
> "The hell with it. I will. Just go ski your easy hills. Maybe
> I'll see you at lunch."

We have frequently seen this type of exchange and have
sympathized with the victim's feelings of worthlessness and
rejection. It is not a pleasant aspect of skiing. Here is an illustra-
tion of how "I"-statements, and your willingness to take re-

sponsibility for your feelings and preferences, may be a way around it.

> "Let's go over and ski Drainpipe."
> "Thanks for the invitation, but I prefer to stay here on this run. I'll meet you later if you want."
> "Aw, c'mon."
> "I really enjoy this run, and I prefer to stay here right now. I would like to meet you in a little while, though."
> "You're chicken."
> "I can't help it if you think that, but I do enjoy skiing over here."
> "O.K. See you in thirty minutes. Have fun!"

And all's well that ends well. Both skiers feel better about each other, their skiing, and, most important, themselves.

WHEN YOU CAN'T DO IT BUT HAVE TO: P.R.A.Y.!

So you have no choice. You got suckered or stumbled onto an unrealistically difficult hill. You think it is a matter of survival. You against the mountain. Your fear is growing. Your mouth is dry. You're thinking, "This is horrible. Just awful. If I don't break something here, it'll be a miracle." You are there, however. The question now is: How can you use your psychology to (1) get down, and (2) *not* resensitize yourself in terms of either fear or anger? One thing is for sure. It is again going to be Mountain—50, Brains—0, if you keep that up.

Here is what you should do. It is a straightforward application of tactics you should already know. The only difference is that you will be using them at a time when it will seem difficult to get it together enough to even remember them, so we have an acronym to make it easier: P.R.A.Y.

> P. = PAUSE for several minutes. Stop rehearsing catastrophes. Stop visualizing falls. Stop looking at poor skiers. (Either look elsewhere or observe and *feel with* a good skier.)
> R. = RELAX. Just take a few deep breaths, letting the crisp air into your lungs, feeling calm.

A. = ANSWER your disastrous self-talk with coping self-statements. Some examples:

"O.K., I'm here. I can take this a couple of turns at a time. Good."

"I have stayed relaxed before. I can do it a couple of turns at a time on this hill, too. It won't feel great, but I'll feel better than I would otherwise have expected."

"I do feel more relaxed. This is just what would be expected—that normal tension and stiffening, which is not *me.* The hill is just more difficult than I'm used to. There, I'm doing fine."

Y. = YOU. Covertly rehearse *you* within the skin of a good skier. Visualize and feel that skier, not the "catastrophe" of falling. Do that every time you pause and relax, but *do not evaluate yourself against that skier.*

If you are coping, you are almost certainly not resensitizing! You are doing fine. It will not be long before you *can* do it.

EXERCISES

1. Practice with a friend (or in your imagination) a couple of dialogues in which you use "I"-statements to say no with grace.
2. Know the P.R.A.Y. acronym, thinking up a couple of answers (counters) that will work *for you.* Don't set yourself up to need it, however. That will happen soon enough, and you will be glad to see how effective it is at that time.

CHAPTER 15

Helping the Heads
of Your Friends

For the most part, we have been addressing skiing as though it were a solitary sport. To be sure, only you are responsible for your skiing. It is your head and your body that turn your skis or lose your balance. The explanations, processes, and exercises we've suggested are for you to do alone so that you can become aware of your own experience. But most people like to ski with someone else. Even if they start the day alone, they are usually happy to meet someone of comparable ability and take a few runs together. If you are a solitary skier, you won't have much use for this chapter. But if you like to ski with other people, you may have a few problems that we want to address here.

First of all, if you're using the suggestions in this book when you ski, your friends are going to ask such questions as, "Why don't you stop where the rest of us stop anymore? We're always stopping at the crest of each pitch, but you always ski right over the edge. Has our deodorant failed us or something?" Or they might say, "You've sure been doing some weird things today. Every time we're about to start off down the slope, you say, 'Wait a second,' and close your eyes. What are you doing, anyway? Praying?" If you haven't already done so, you'd better let your friends know what you are doing. Without any explanation, they may take your behavior personally. Or they may decide that you've finally lost your marbles.

We wouldn't want you to lose any friends because you've found some tactics that help you ski better.

In addition to explaining the processes that you're using so they won't think you're a little strange, there are some things you can do to make their skiing more fun. Obviously, if they're interested in the whole from-the-head-down approach, we have no objection to your giving them a copy of this book. On the other hand, we're not suggesting that you proselytize. Don't take the "holier than thou" approach. This is not a belief system or a religious movement. It is merely a series of principles that work. Which means that you can make them work for your friends by what you *do* with your friends.

BEING A MODEL

Skiers can learn a lot by observing and imitating each other. However, unless you're a ski instructor, you may not feel comfortable modeling ski *technique* for your friends. On the other hand, whether you like it or not, you are modeling an *attitude* toward skiing.

As you know, emotions are contagious. If you are experiencing joy, it will be easier for your friends to be happy with their own skiing. On the other hand, if you are experiencing fear or frustration, your friends may pick up on those emotions—unless they know enough to ignore you. Let's assume that they don't. You already know some ways of handling those emotions if they should arise. If you are at the point where you can cope with the feeling quickly and efficiently, you probably will not be affecting your friends adversely. In fact, they will probably learn something from observing you. However, if your negative emotions are controlling you, and not the other way around, you can do your friends a favor by staying away from them temporarily.

BEING YOUR FRIENDS' "OWN BEST FRIEND"

You can also do some things to help your friends when they are having a bad day. What has been your typical reaction to a frustrated friend? "Friends" usually make one of three responses, none of which is particularly helpful. One is to be sympathetic:

> "Dammit! I can't ski this stuff. I'm so discouraged."
> "Yeah. You look like you're not doing too well at all. Is there anything I can do to help?"
> "No, no. I just feel miserable. I don't know what's wrong. Maybe I should just quit for the day."

The "friend" has good intentions, but the sympathy only discourages the skier more.

The second response is commiseration:

> "Dammit! I can't ski this stuff. I'm so discouraged."
> "I know what you mean. I'm having a terrible time, too. Just look at me. I can't do anything right. I'm skiing as badly as you are. These conditions are terrible."
> "I know, I know. I sometimes think that I hate this sport. Maybe we should *both* quit for the day."

Misery loves company, right? Not exactly. Social psychology research shows that misery loves *miserable* company. If you want to truly share a friend's misery, you have to get miserable, too. Are you ready for that? Even if you do become miserable yourself, you won't be helping your friend. Commiseration doesn't provide any useful ways of getting out of the misery. In fact, it just reinforces it.

The third response is to deny the friend's experience altogether by being complimentary:

> "Dammit! I can't ski this stuff. I'm so discouraged."
> "Gee, I don't see why. You're skiing really nicely. You look great!"
> "No, I don't. Did you see those last turns? I was terrible, awful. Maybe I should quit for the day."
> "Oh, no. Don't do that. Honest, you really look good. In fact, you look as good as anyone up here."
> "Oh, really?"

This last exchange is particularly insidious. Many skiers have gotten into the habit of berating themselves precisely *because* they thereby elicit complimentary responses from others. To make things worse, this motivation is usually unconscious. People are usually unaware that they are into this negative habit. They don't even know that their friends are unwittingly reinforcing the complaining. Nor do their friends know. Of course, as this pattern is repeated, the friends eventually stop being complimentary and stay away from their complaining companion. By then the pattern is well established, and the unfortunate skier is left with the negative self-statements— which he or she has come to believe completely!

If you respond to a friend's complaints in any of these three ways, you are not unusual. Each of the above responses carries the best intentions. The problem is that none of them will actually help your friend's skiing. On the other hand, this doesn't mean you should say nothing. That will just turn your friend away. The most constructive things you can say follow from the principles in this book. If your friend is having a bad day and is berating himself for his skiing, consider a dialogue like the following:

"Dammit! I can't ski this stuff. I'm so discouraged."

"Sounds like you're talking yourself into it. I'd feel pretty discouraged, too, if I talked to myself like that."

"Well, I just get so frustrated. I can't do anything right. I'll never be a good skier."

"If you say so, you probably won't. You're fighting yourself *and* your skiing."

"I guess I am, but I can't help myself. The words just came out. I don't know what else to do."

"I have a few suggestions if you don't mind my playing 'teacher.' "

"No, I can use all the help I can get."

"Well, first of all, see what happens if you talk to yourself more realistically. You know it's not that you *can't* ski this stuff or that you'll *never* be any good. It's just that you're falling a lot today."

"Yeah, so?"

"So what's the big deal about falling? That's part of skiing. Everyone falls."

"I guess that's true. But I get so *tense* when I fall. Then I tighten up and ski miserably."

"And fall some more."

"Right. But what can I do?"

"I have some exercises that helped me with that. I'll show you if you want. In the meantime, see if you can notice something nice about your skiing from here to the bottom. Even if you fall again, notice what you like about your falls. I'll explain more on the way back up."

"O.K. That might be fun. Thanks."

Naturally, your dialogue may not go like this one. Your friend may not want to hear your observations or may want to argue with you, as if to convince you that he or she is not any good. In response to that, all you can do is shrug your shoulders and say, "O.K., if you insist that you can't ski, then I guess you can't."

Before we go on, we want to acknowledge one way that many people have unwittingly become their friends' "own worst enemy." Typically, this occurs when one person knows the terrain ahead and the others don't. The first skier attempts to "help" the others with a few words of warning about the potential catastrophes just around the corner. In trying to forewarn their friends of difficulties ahead, this person succeeds only in generating a lot of fear. The usual comments go something like this: "Watch out over the next knoll. It's really rocky and icy. You probably want to take it easy. If you fall, you slide all the way to the bottom. I saw a guy get really scraped up there last weekend. Had to get a toboggan and everything!" With friends like that, who needs enemies? If a friend is going to say anything at all, a more useful comment is: "The next pitch has some ice and rocks in it. I usually find it's best if you stay way over to the right side." This statement not only does not catastrophize but also provides some practical information.

HELPING YOUR FRIENDS TO S.K.I.

As you are aware, there is more to skiing from the head down than correcting your friends' self-talk. Your friends probably have not developed much active awareness about their skiing. So if you really want to help them, that's where to start.

When they say, "I can't do it," you should ask, "Can't do what?" Are they talking about skiing bumps, holding on ice, relaxing, falling, being good to themselves—or what? In other words, what are the specific problems? The next question to ask is: "Why can't you do it?" Specifically, what are the inner and outer contexts that contribute to the problems? Ask them the same questions that you ask yourself when you "S.K.I." Your purpose in asking them of your friends is to *help them refine their frustration down to something workable.* It is to help them go from amorphous goals like "skiing better" or "having fun" to specifics like "relaxing in the bumps" or "saying nice things to myself, especially when I fall." Once they have distilled their problems down into realistic units, they will be in a position to use the principles in this book to help themselves. No magic, no mysticism. Just a little psychology.

DO'S AND DON'TS

DO'S

- *Do* let your friends know what you're doing if you're practicing the exercises in this book.
- *Do* share your joy, if that is what you are experiencing.
- *Do* ask your friends' permission if you want to comment on their ski psychology.
- After *they* fall, *do* make sure they are using the time to covertly rehearse their next few turns and are not catastrophizing.
- *Do* help them specify their frustrations into something manageable.
- *Do* notice the differences in your rhythms, and respect those differences.

DON'TS

- *Don't* proselytize about this book or its principles. They are neither sacred nor magical.
- *Don't* be sympathetic, commiserating, or compli-

mentary if your friends berate themselves. You are giving them no new information, only a payoff to continue their complaints.

- *Don't* share your frustrations if you're being "your own worst enemy." Keep your "enemies" to yourself.
- *Don't* catastrophize to your friends in an effort to warn them of difficult terrain.
- *Don't* beat your drum to your friends' rhythm—or ask your friends to beat theirs to your rhythm.

CHAPTER 16

Exercise from the Head Down

To ski well and enjoy it, you must be in shape. To get (or stay) in shape for skiing takes some effort. For most people, it always takes effort to work toward a somewhat vague benefit somewhere in the future. Every day seems to be that rainy day. You "might as well" just watch TV and have a drink. Exercise may be well rewarded on the mountain, but it "hurts like hell" while you are forcing yourself to do it. We would like to make it easier for you to get in shape for skiing.

Physical exercise is a behavior, just as skiing is a behavior. For most people, however, it is a low-probability behavior. You "know" you should exercise, but you "just can't seem to make yourself do it." If that fits, or if you are an *ex*-exerciser (perhaps a jogging dropout), this chapter is for you. If you do exercise regularly and consider yourself in good shape, you are probably already (perhaps unwittingly) using the principles we discuss in this chapter.

PSYCHOLOGY AND EXERCISE

The psychology of human learning that we have applied to skiing also applies to exercise. First, your behavior doesn't pop up out of nowhere, nor is it "driven" by hidden forces (though without active awareness it is typical to feel that it is).

170

Second, the feelings you have about moguls, powder, or exercise are part of your emotional learning and do interact with your operant learning. Like skiing, exercise is an operant (it is voluntary). Third, certain payoffs maintain or increase the probability of certain behaviors, while others decrease that probability. The probability of exercise is low for many people, and that is a problem.

REASONS WHY YOU SHOULDN'T

You say you do not exercise, but wish you could. What are your excuses?

> "Can't seem to find the time."
> "I hate jogging."
> "I'm so out of shape—why bother?"
> "I get all sweaty."
> "No place to go."
> "I'd make my friends feel guilty."

An "excuse" is anything that, in your opinion, decreases the probability of exercise. It might be something unpleasant (like getting all sweaty) or something *more* pleasant that you would do instead (like sitting around and reading the paper).

Now if you are serious about wishing to exercise, you are going to have to make a serious effort at active awareness and at changing some of your payoffs. You may as well begin now by taking out a paper and pencil and getting down to work. (If this strikes you as too much effort, we can't help you.)

Make an exhaustive and detailed list of your excuses. Not "I hate jogging," but exactly what you hate about jogging. Not "I end up with no time in the day," but exactly what you find yourself doing that consumes the day. Not "I'd rather do something else," but exactly what else you would rather do—for example, relax for thirty minutes with nobody around. This is the first step in your active awareness. Isn't it true that "reasons why you shouldn't" are nothing more than excuses?

REASONS WHY YOU SHOULD

Now make a second list, an exhaustive and sincere tally of reasons why you should exercise. They should be believable to you; you should really understand and mean each one of them. Not "So I can be a long-distance runner" (at least not for most of us!), but "I will feel better about my body and about myself." Not "So I'll never have a heart attack," but "So that my chances of a fatal heart attack will be decreased" or "To tone up my cardiovascular system." Examples:

> "I'll be able to have longer days on the mountain."
> "I won't have to stop so often on bump runs."
> "I won't be so out of breath when I ski higher elevations."
> "I'll probably sleep better."
> "I'll feel better about myself and my body."

WHERE YOU ARE NOW

One effective payoff is *seeing* some change in your behavior and/or your body. Note a few things for your records. How often are you exercising now, if at all? What is the duration of your exercise period? Chart it if you wish. (If your exercise rate is zero or very low, it should be no problem for you to remember and note down the history of the past two weeks.) What is your resting pulse after five minutes of sitting quietly? While standing (orthostatic tolerance)? After a "standard" exercise? After recovery? (Check some of the widely available exercise books, or consult a physician or exercise physiologist.) These will change with cardiovascular conditioning.

You may also be exercising to lose weight. Do not try to use your weight as a baseline. Exercise is only half the weight-control formula. The other half is caloric intake, and we are not addressing that issue here. (If you wish to do some weight management, we highly recommend a book that applies to weight control many of the same principles discussed in this book: M. J. Mahoney and K. Mahoney, *Permanent Weight Control: A Total Solution to the Dieter's Dilemma* [New York: W. W. Norton, 1976].)

Keep your log as a check on how much you are exercising.

It is gratifying to see (and feel) that increasing exercise results in increased stamina. When walking a mile was tough and you are now running two, that is a measurable and reinforcing result.

YOUR INNER CONTEXTS AND EXERCISE

As in skiing, there are both inner and outer contexts for you to consider. Your inner contexts have to do with not "feeling" like exercising, "feeling guilty" if you don't, making up excuses, and goal-setting. Several of these are rooted in your self-talk. Modify some of your self-talk, and you will begin to modify much of the way you "feel" about your exercise.

An example is the standard-setting issue. Especially if you have not been exercising, you may feel as though working your way back into shape will take forever. So your self-talk may include the "what's-the-use" theme. Alternatively, you may start a program of exercise and find no significant change after two weeks. This is setting yourself up for disappointment and an excuse to quit. As in the Self-defeating Syndrome, you may find yourself saying, "Well, that just goes to show you. Exercise doesn't do a bit of good for me. Besides, my body aches." What needs changing are your expectations and your self-talk.

You may also feel guilty when you fail to exercise. Watching a gaggle of self-righteous joggers, complains a friend of ours, is nauseating. When we inquired what he meant by that, he said it made him feel somewhat guilty because he "knew" that he should be doing it. Feeling guilty, then, may be conceptualized as a bunch of "oughts" or "shoulds." "I 'ought' to be exercising." "I really 'should' quit sitting around with my Scotch and water every night." Such statements lead more often to resentment than to exercise.

Applying S.E.L.F.-modification techniques to work with your inner contexts is also an integral part of starting and maintaining your exercise program. We will briefly review them as they apply here:

STOP. Stop your self-talk about "oughts" and "shoulds."

Stop discussing, with yourself or anyone else, your aches, being out of breath, and other physiological changes that you "suffer" with exercise.

EVALUATE. What kind of expectations do you have? Are you expecting to see a major change in your body? Expecting to run three miles a day with little effort? These would be self-defeating ideas, obviously. Instead, your expectations should be that you will *begin* to feel better. You will get a cardiovascular training effect after several months, not several weeks.

LABEL. One area that can use some conscientious work is your labeling of those aches and pains. Instead of excuses to quit, they are (within reason) evidence that you can use the workout. You *will* be out of breath, and your pulse *will* increase significantly. Without this, there would be no cardiovascular conditioning. The appropriate label would take that fact into account—for example, "I am making an investment now to make it easier in the future." Remember, labeling is your own undertaking. Make up "counters" that work best for you.

FOLLOW UP. This one is particularly important. How do you feel about yourself after exercise? Good? Say so! Pat yourself on the back. Look at yourself in the mirror and say, "Good! I am doing great! I am feeling better." Exercise is often a lonely undertaking, so *self*-praise should be considered an integral part of your effort. Also, covert rehearsal can act as a payoff. For example, imagine yourself skiing with more stamina and more breath control. Do this both as you are exercising and at other times you are tempted to quit. Temptations, after all, are nothing more than self-statements that are mostly rationalizations or excuses.

YOUR OUTER CONTEXTS AND EXERCISE

Some of the most powerful outer contexts influencing your exercise (or lack of it) are activities that *compete* with exercise. When you don't work out because you "don't have time" or because "it doesn't feel good," you must be aware of what you are doing instead. There is an excellent way to *use* competing activities to *increase* the probability of exercise. You can then turn your excuses to your advantage. It is simple: do not permit yourself your favored activity *until* you have met your exercise goal for that day. Why should you want to do something as apparently perverse and masochistic as that? The answer is straightforward. What you are doing is letting the higher-probability activity function as a payoff for the lower-probability activity (exercise).

There are two points to remember about this tactic: be sure you are careful in your analysis of what is competing with exercise, and be consistent in your use of the technique.

Shaping

Be gradual. Let's suppose you are going to jog as one of your exercises. Work up to it. First, walk a distance shorter than your final goal. Then, walk partway and jog partway. Finally, jog the entire distance, decreasing the time and increasing the distance. During this process, be sure to use self-praise at each step!

If you just "can't make yourself do it" one day—and that is bound to happen from time to time—*do not* punish yourself. Instead, be sure to at least walk the distance. Once you get out there, you have significantly increased the probability of jogging all or part of the way. But the point is that your old competing activities are not sneaking in again. Make your goals realistic and shape your way toward them, whether you are jogging, taking a YMCA exercise course, or engaging in a workout at your club.

A Little Help from Your Friends

Your friends are an outer context, too. They do not have to be exercisers themselves to help you in your program. If they are, you can be mutually supportive and enjoy each other while exercising. But friends who are *not* involved can also be of great help. They can be supportive and encourage you to keep with your program—*if* they know what you're undertaking and how you're progressing.

Make a chart of your exercise time and post it on the refrigerator or the inside of your office door. Make it public, so that your friends and colleagues will know how you are doing. Ask for a "good word" from them as they see you sticking to your plan. (Don't forget to let the chart be a cue for you to give a good word to yourself, of course!) You could even arrange for them to fine you if you go off schedule. Though we much prefer to "accentuate the positive," you may find that such a penalty works for you. It does for many people.

ON BECOMING A DROPOUT

If you begin your exercise program with the goals of an idealist and the passion of a New Year's resolutionist, you are setting yourself up for trouble. If you resist that temptation, you are significantly decreasing your chances of becoming an exercise dropout. But let us suppose you undertake a reasonable program and run into trouble. Here is a checklist:

1. Is your self-talk supportive? Do you "want" to exercise—if you could only "make yourself"? Or are you saying you "really ought" to exercise? The latter is a bit more difficult to work with. Search again for supportive reasons. Write them down. Remind yourself of them several times a day. And after your workout, give yourself plenty of praise!
2. Are your goals realistic? Some exercise is better than none.
3. Is there another activity competing for the time you've set aside for exercise, one that you find irresistible when you are honest with yourself? If so, pick another time and an activity you *can* postpone and subsequently *earn* for yourself. *Be consistent.*
4. Are you shaping your exercising as you move toward your personal goal? If you find yourself increasingly missing your sessions, drop back a little and work back up. The program may be too pun-

ishing for you at that level. But note that you *will* have to do some pushing in order to benefit.

We intentionally make no recommendations about the exercise program itself. There have been many books published on the subject, and ski magazines usually offer suggestions each year. Also, most Y's, athletic clubs, and health spas have regularly scheduled group programs, even some specially designed for skiers. If you keep at it, exercise can "get you in touch with your body," much as skiing does. It can also create some of the same peak experiences.

EXERCISE

Exercise!

CHAPTER 17

Transcendence

S.K.I.ing and P.R.A.Y.ing . . . relaxing . . . rehearsing . . . your music . . . your metaphors . . . your rhythm . . . your falls . . . your friends . . . your own worst enemy . . . your own best friend . . . your S.E.L.F. . . . from the head down. How does it all fit together? There is a right-brain and a left-brain answer to that.

First, the linear, logical, left-brain answer. Using the S.K.I. approach to active awareness, you identified your strengths and weaknesses and set some specific objectives for improvement. It wasn't magic, and it wasn't mysticism. Working with the tactics in this book, you approached your problems positively and systematically. You relaxed, you coped with your frustrations, you dealt with your anger. You let yourself SENSE, and you found that the work of skiing from the head down was fun. So you extended yourself, seeking new personal challenges. You played with images and rhythms. You improved your concentration. You discovered two of your own best friends: you *and* the mountain. The challenge remains. You continue to improve, and you find joy in doing one thing better today than you did yesterday. You take satisfaction in using your head.

Now the holistic, experiential, right-brain answer. You pursued the suggestions in this book and experienced the joy of improvement. Then one day you find you are skiing *without* thinking about tactics—or anything else, for that matter. You are totally immersed. Nothing exists except the sense of grace, of oneness with the mountain, and a single clear note ringing in your head. In a letter to his long-time skiing friend Charles Lobitz, the Canadian poet Claude Liman wrote of a peak experience, of his awareness of

> my brother's exquisite motion down the slope; I push off and follow in his wake, beneath the double chair where people are still leaning out to admire how he goes. Suddenly I am young again and the people are leaning out to watch me, too. There is sun on a wide expanse of trail, all of it flowing downhill with me riding it like a chip in a current. I don't really have to move. Motion is around me, and I am carried. Moguls are waves which can only be negotiated by instinct, by launching oneself into the pattern and learning the maze by sheer reaction. I do not turn so much as push off each ledge, then the next and the next, reversing when the ground comes up to be a platform for my next impulse. I never could make good turns on slopes the snowcats have groomed into boredom. I must feel I am unlocking a mystery with each reaction to minute pieces of new terrain. Certain runs have that inevitable quality of destiny, when sunlight and snow and air and me and a path through the moguls intersect at that auspicious moment. Motion is the catalyst.

You finish the run in a state of ecstasy: "My God, that was incredible!" When you return home, you think back through this book, trying to recall the chapter on *that* experience. You would like to make it happen again.

But the chapter doesn't exist. There are no psychological instructions for a peak experience. It doesn't work that way. All of the systematic exercises, all of the work, and all of the fun of skiing from the head down came together in that one beautiful moment. At that point—a point in space, perhaps, or time—there was an intangible merging of thinking and experiencing.

So you go back to working on your challenges, taking satisfaction in using your head, sensing, inquiring, knowing that the experience will come again. You go back to the end of Chapter 1 . . .

. . . to let go, to feel, to be aware of your relationship with the mountain in space and time. It fits together as an entire experience, a Gestalt, an integration of your body and mind that, when working right, seems spiritual in its beauty and grace. It is an intense individual challenge, a communication between a lone skier and a mountain that is itself as complex in variety as you are in your feelings and thoughts and ways of skiing.

Selected Bibliography

Bandura, A. *Social Learning Theory.* Englewood Cliffs, N.J.: Prentice-Hall, 1977.

Bem, S. L. "Verbal Self-Control: The Establishment of Effective Self-Instruction." *Journal of Experimental Psychology* 74 (1967): 485–491.

Bernstein, D. A., and Borkovec, T. D. *Progressive Relaxation: A Manual for Therapists.* Champaign, Ill.: Research Press, 1973.

Ellis, A. *Reason and Emotion in Psychotherapy.* New York: Lyle Stuart, 1962.

Farber, I. E. "The Things People Say to Themselves." *American Psychologist* 18 (1963): 185–197.

Gallwey, W. T. *The Inner Game of Tennis.* New York: Random House, 1974.

Jacobson, E. *Progressive Relaxation.* Chicago: University of Chicago Press, 1938.

Kazdin, A. E. "Covert Modeling, Model Similarity, and Reduction of Avoidance Behavior." *Behavior Therapy* 5 (1974): 325–340.

Kidd, B., and Hall, D. K. *Ski in Six Days.* Chicago: Henry Regnery, 1975.

Lawther, J. D. *Sport Psychology.* Englewood Cliffs, N.J.: Prentice-Hall, 1972.

Mahoney, M. J. *Cognition and Behavior Modification.* Cambridge, Mass.: Ballinger, 1974.

Meichenbaum, D. "Cognitive Factors in Behavior Modification: Modifying What Clients Say to Themselves." In *Annual Review of Behavior Therapy, Theory and Practice,* vol. 1, edited by C. M. Franks and G. T. Wilson, pp. 416–431. New York: Brunner/Mazel, 1973.

————. *Cognitive-Behavior Modification.* New York: Plenum Publishing Corp., 1977.

————. "Self-Instructional Methods." In *Helping People Change,* edited by F. Kanfer and A. Goldstein. New York: Pergamon Press, 1975.

Nideffer, R. M. *The Inner Athlete: Mind Plus Muscle for Winning.* New York: Crowell, 1976.

Ornstein, R. E. *The Psychology of Consciousness.* San Francisco: W. H. Freeman, 1971.

Paul, G. L., and Bernstein, D. A. *Anxiety and Behavior: Treatment by Systematic Desensitization and Related Techniques.* New York: General Learning Press, 1973.

Pelletier, K. *Mind as Healer, Mind as Slayer.* New York: Delacorte Press, 1977.

Richardson, A. "Mental Practice: A Review and Discussion." *Research Quarterly* 38 (1967): Part 1, 95–107; Part 2, 263–272.

Rimm, D. C., and Litvak, S. B. "Self-Verbalization and Emotional Arousal." *Journal of Abnormal Psychology* 74 (1969): 181–187.

Schachter, S., and Singer, J. E. "Cognitive, Social, and Physiological Determinants of Emotional State." *Psychological Review* 69 (1962): 379–399.

Sherman, A. R. "Real-Life Exposure as a Primary Therapeutic Factor in the Desensitization Treatment of Fear." *Journal of Abnormal Psychology* 79 (1972): 19–28.

Singer, J. L. *Imagery and Daydream Methods in Psychotherapy and Behavior Modification.* New York: Academic Press, 1974.

Singer, R. N. *Myths and Truths in Sports Psychology.* New York: Harper & Row, 1975.

Smith, M. J. *When I Say No I Feel Guilty.* New York: Dial Press, 1975.

Sperry, R. W. "Hemisphere Deconnection and Unity in Conscious Awareness." *American Psychologist* 23 (1968): 723–733.

Suinn, R. M. "Removing Emotional Obstacles to Learning and Performance by Visuo-Motor Behavior Rehearsal." *Behavior Therapy* 3 (1972): 308–310.

———. "Behavior Rehearsal Training for Ski Racers." *Behavior Therapy* 3 (1972): 519–520.

———. "Behavioral Methods at the Winter Olympic Games." *Behavior Therapy* 8 (1977): 283–284.

Thoresen, C. E., and Mahoney, M. J. *Behavioral Self-Control.* New York: Holt, Rinehart & Winston, 1974.

About the Authors

LEONARD A. LOUDIS, Ed.D., who holds his doctorate in psychology, began skiing a few years ago in the Colorado Rockies. As he learned, he accelerated his progress by systematic application of the psychological principles he now writes about. An Assistant Professor of Psychology at Metropolitan State College in Denver, he also leads numerous workshops in the western United States.

W. CHARLES LOBITZ, Ph.D., is an Assistant Professor of Psychology at the University of Colorado Medical School in Denver. He began to ski when he was four years old, was a three-year letterman in skiing at Dartmouth College and a top slalom and giant slalom racer in the East from 1964 to 1967, and later became a university ski coach. In addition to teaching and a practice in clinical psychology, he conducts workshops and publishes many professional papers.